iBelieve
the Unbelievable & Receive the Impossible

Devotional Journal

Jesse Duplantis

iBelieve Devotional Journal
ISBN 978-0-9819977-2-8
Copyright © 2013
by Jesse Duplantis

Published by Jesse Duplantis Ministries
PO Box 1089
Destrehan, Louisiana 70047
USA
985-764-2000
www.jdm.org

Jesse Duplantis Ministries is dedicated to reaching people and changing lives with the Gospel of Jesus Christ. For more information, or to purchase other products from Jesse Duplantis Ministries, please contact us at the address above.

Printed in the United States of America. All rights reserved under International Copyright Law. Contents and/or cover may not be reproduced in whole or in part in any form without the express written consent of the Publisher.

What Are You Believing For?

I Believe... these two little words have the power to change your future. They are the starting point for the life you want—the life God means for you to live. The *iBelieve Devotional Journal* is a place to write those "unbelievable" and "impossible" thoughts and dreams you have inside of you, and a place to document when those same things come to pass.

Use it to write Scripture-based confessions that apply to your situation. Use it to jot down the important points you hear from teachers, preachers, or friends that encourage you to keep moving forward. Use it jot down what the Holy Spirit reveals to you about yourself and His Word during your times of study and prayer.

There is a greater life for you, and it begins when you realize that *everything* God asks you to believe is *un*believable. It's ALL impossible...that's why it's called faith! So, if you are going to believe, why not believe for what's really in your heart of hearts? Why not stretch the limits of what you think you "can" and "cannot" do? Why not read this scripture below and not only believe it, but start working on bringing it to pass?

"For verily I say unto you, That whosoever shall say unto this mountain, Be thou removed, and be thou cast into the sea; and shall not doubt in his heart, but shall believe that those things which he saith shall come to pass; he shall have whatsoever he saith" (Mark 11:23). Those are the words of Jesus Christ and they are the very definition of "believing the unbelievable and receiving the impossible." And, yet, Christ told us that this is something we CAN do!

The *iBelieve Devotional Journal* is a place to remind yourself that you CAN: You *can* move mountainous problems with your words of faith...You *can* break free from what is holding you down or holding you back...You *can* move forward and not only *accomplish* what you set your mind to, but also *have* what you set your FAITH to!

God is for you; He is not against you! Put your faith and your words to work as you use this devotional journal to define and document what you and God can do together. Remember, it all starts when you open your heart, stretch the limits, and say, "God...*I BELIEVE!*"

– Jesse Duplantis

**I Will BELIEVE the Unbelievable and RECEIVE the Impossible...
MY POWER IS IN MY SAYING AND BELIEVING!**

_____

_____

_____

_____

_____

_____

_____

_____

_____

_____

_____

_____

_____

_____

_____

_____

_____

_____

_____

_____

_____

_____

_____

_____

_____

*Date Set:*_____ *Date Accomplished/Received:*_____

"For verily I say unto you, That whosoever shall say unto this mountain, Be thou removed, and be thou cast into the sea; and shall not doubt in his heart, but shall believe that those things which he saith shall come to pass; he shall have whatsoever he saith." – **Jesus, Mark 11:23**

_____
_____
_____
_____
_____
_____
_____
_____
_____
_____
_____
_____
_____
_____
_____
_____
_____
_____
_____
_____
_____
_____
_____
_____

Date Set:_____ Date Accomplished/Received:_____

**I Will BELIEVE the Unbelievable and RECEIVE the Impossible…
MY POWER IS IN MY SAYING AND BELIEVING!**

_Date Set:_____ _Date Accomplished/Received:_____

"For verily I say unto you, That whosoever shall say unto this mountain, Be thou removed, and be thou cast into the sea; and shall not doubt in his heart, but shall believe that those things which he saith shall come to pass; he shall have whatsoever he saith." – **Jesus, Mark 11:23**

Date Set:_____ Date Accomplished/Received:_____

**I Will BELIEVE the Unbelievable and RECEIVE the Impossible...
MY POWER IS IN MY SAYING AND BELIEVING!**

_____
_____
_____
_____
_____
_____
_____
_____
_____
_____
_____
_____
_____
_____
_____
_____
_____
_____
_____
_____
_____
_____
_____

*Date Set:*_____ *Date Accomplished/Received:*_____

*"For verily I say unto you, That whosoever shall say unto this mountain, Be thou removed, and be thou cast into the sea; and shall not doubt in his heart, but shall believe that those things which he saith shall come to pass; he shall have whatsoever he saith." – **Jesus, Mark 11:23**_

_____
_____
_____
_____
_____
_____
_____
_____
_____
_____
_____
_____
_____
_____
_____
_____
_____
_____
_____
_____
_____
_____
_____
_____
_____

*Date Set:*_____ *Date Accomplished/Received:*_____

**I Will BELIEVE the Unbelievable and RECEIVE the Impossible…
MY POWER IS IN MY SAYING AND BELIEVING!**

Date Set:_____ Date Accomplished/Received:_____

"For verily I say unto you, That whosoever shall say unto this mountain, Be thou removed, and be thou cast into the sea; and shall not doubt in his heart, but shall believe that those things which he saith shall come to pass; he shall have whatsoever he saith." – **Jesus, Mark 11:23**

_____
_____
_____
_____
_____
_____
_____
_____
_____
_____
_____
_____
_____
_____
_____
_____
_____
_____
_____
_____
_____
_____
_____
_____
_____

Date Set:_____ Date Accomplished/Received:_____

**I Will BELIEVE the Unbelievable and RECEIVE the Impossible...
MY POWER IS IN MY SAYING AND BELIEVING!**

_____

_____

_____

_____

_____

_____

_____

_____

_____

_____

_____

_____

_____

_____

_____

_____

_____

_____

_____

_____

_____

_____

_____

*Date Set:*_____ *Date Accomplished/Received:*_____

*"For verily I say unto you, That whosoever shall say unto this mountain, Be thou removed, and be thou cast into the sea; and shall not doubt in his heart, but shall believe that those things which he saith shall come to pass; he shall have whatsoever he saith." – **Jesus, Mark 11:23**

_____
_____
_____
_____
_____
_____
_____
_____
_____
_____
_____
_____
_____
_____
_____
_____
_____
_____
_____
_____
_____
_____
_____
_____
_____
_____
_____

Date Set:_____ Date Accomplished/Received:_____

**I Will BELIEVE the Unbelievable and RECEIVE the Impossible…
MY POWER IS IN MY SAYING AND BELIEVING!**

_Date Set:_____ _Date Accomplished/Received:_____

Make a plan for yourself to study the Word. (2 Timothy 2:15)

Make it your first priority. Remember, you are creating your future not by what you read in the Word, but by what you *know* and *use* from God's Word (2 Timothy 1:12). Faith is something I like to call spiritualized common sense. Never think with just your natural mind; think with the Word of God.

I Will BELIEVE the Unbelievable and RECEIVE the Impossible...
MY POWER IS IN MY SAYING AND BELIEVING!

_____

_____

_____

_____

_____

_____

_____

_____

_____

_____

_____

_____

_____

_____

_____

_____

_____

_____

_____

_____

_____

_____

_____

_____

*Date Set:*_____ *Date Accomplished/Received:*_____

*"For verily I say unto you, That whosoever shall say unto this mountain, Be thou removed, and be thou cast into the sea; and shall not doubt in his heart, but shall believe that those things which he saith shall come to pass; he shall have whatsoever he saith." – **Jesus, Mark 11:23***

_____
_____
_____
_____
_____
_____
_____
_____
_____
_____
_____
_____
_____
_____
_____
_____
_____
_____
_____
_____
_____
_____
_____
_____

*Date Set:*_____ *Date Accomplished/Received:*_____

**I Will BELIEVE the Unbelievable and RECEIVE the Impossible...
MY POWER IS IN MY SAYING AND BELIEVING!**

_____

_____

_____

_____

_____

_____

_____

_____

_____

_____

_____

_____

_____

_____

_____

_____

_____

_____

_____

_____

_____

_____

_____

_____

*Date Set:*_____ *Date Accomplished/Received:*_____

*"For verily I say unto you, That whosoever shall say unto this mountain, Be thou removed, and be thou cast into the sea; and shall not doubt in his heart, but shall believe that those things which he saith shall come to pass; he shall have whatsoever he saith." – **Jesus, Mark 11:23***

_____

_____

_____

_____

_____

_____

_____

_____

_____

_____

_____

_____

_____

_____

_____

_____

_____

_____

_____

_____

_____

_____

*Date Set:*_____ *Date Accomplished/Received:*_____

**I Will BELIEVE the Unbelievable and RECEIVE the Impossible…
MY POWER IS IN MY SAYING AND BELIEVING!**

_____
_____
_____
_____
_____
_____
_____
_____
_____
_____
_____
_____
_____
_____
_____
_____
_____
_____
_____
_____
_____
_____
_____

*Date Set:*_____ *Date Accomplished/Received:*_____

*"For verily I say unto you, That whosoever shall say unto this mountain, Be thou removed, and be thou cast into the sea; and shall not doubt in his heart, but shall believe that those things which he saith shall come to pass; he shall have whatsoever he saith." – **Jesus, Mark 11:23***

_____

_____

_____

_____

_____

_____

_____

_____

_____

_____

_____

_____

_____

_____

_____

_____

_____

_____

_____

_____

_____

_____

_____

_____

_____

_____

_____

_____

*Date Set:*_____ *Date Accomplished/Received:*_____

**I Will BELIEVE the Unbelievable and RECEIVE the Impossible...
MY POWER IS IN MY SAYING AND BELIEVING!**

Date Set:_____ Date Accomplished/Received:_____

*"For verily I say unto you, That whosoever shall say unto this mountain, Be thou removed, and be thou cast into the sea; and shall not doubt in his heart, but shall believe that those things which he saith shall come to pass; he shall have whatsoever he saith." – **Jesus, Mark 11:23***

_____

_____

_____

_____

_____

_____

_____

_____

_____

_____

_____

_____

_____

_____

_____

_____

_____

_____

_____

_____

_____

_____

_____

_____

_____

*Date Set:*_____ *Date Accomplished/Received:*_____

**I Will BELIEVE the Unbelievable and RECEIVE the Impossible…
MY POWER IS IN MY SAYING AND BELIEVING!**

Date Set:_____ Date Accomplished/Received:_____

*"For verily I say unto you, That whosoever shall say unto this mountain, Be thou removed, and be thou cast into the sea; and shall not doubt in his heart, but shall believe that those things which he saith shall come to pass; he shall have whatsoever he saith." – **Jesus, Mark 11:23**

_____
_____
_____
_____
_____
_____
_____
_____
_____
_____
_____
_____
_____
_____
_____
_____
_____
_____
_____
_____
_____
_____
_____
_____
_____

*Date Set:*_____ *Date Accomplished/Received:*_____

I Will BELIEVE the Unbelievable and RECEIVE the Impossible…
MY POWER IS IN MY SAYING AND BELIEVING!

_____
_____
_____
_____
_____
_____
_____
_____
_____
_____
_____
_____
_____
_____
_____
_____
_____
_____
_____
_____
_____
_____

*Date Set:*_____ *Date Accomplished/Received:*_____

Everything we are told to believe God about or for is *unbelievable* and *impossible*.

The whole of Scripture has nothing to do with what we can do by ourselves. It pushes us to stretch beyond our natural mind and what our natural senses can grasp…to break free from a mere religious mind and become what I like to call "God-inside minded."

**I Will BELIEVE the Unbelievable and RECEIVE the Impossible...
MY POWER IS IN MY SAYING AND BELIEVING!**

_____

_____

_____

_____

_____

_____

_____

_____

_____

_____

_____

_____

_____

_____

_____

_____

_____

_____

_____

_____

*Date Set:*_____ *Date Accomplished/Received:*_____

*"For verily I say unto you, That whosoever shall say unto this mountain, Be thou removed, and be thou cast into the sea; and shall not doubt in his heart, but shall believe that those things which he saith shall come to pass; he shall have whatsoever he saith." – **Jesus, Mark 11:23***

Date Set:_____ Date Accomplished/Received:_____

**I Will BELIEVE the Unbelievable and RECEIVE the Impossible...
MY POWER IS IN MY SAYING AND BELIEVING!**

_Date Set:_____ _Date Accomplished/Received:_____

*"For verily I say unto you, That whosoever shall say unto this mountain, Be thou removed, and be thou cast into the sea; and shall not doubt in his heart, but shall believe that those things which he saith shall come to pass; he shall have whatsoever he saith." – **Jesus, Mark 11:23**†

_____

_____

_____

_____

_____

_____

_____

_____

_____

_____

_____

_____

_____

_____

_____

_____

_____

_____

_____

_____

_____

_____

_____

*Date Set:*_____ *Date Accomplished/Received:*_____

**I Will BELIEVE the Unbelievable and RECEIVE the Impossible...
MY POWER IS IN MY SAYING AND BELIEVING!**

_____
_____
_____
_____
_____
_____
_____
_____
_____
_____
_____
_____
_____
_____
_____
_____
_____
_____
_____
_____
_____
_____
_____

Date Set:_____ Date Accomplished/Received:_____

*"For verily I say unto you, That whosoever shall say unto this mountain, Be thou removed, and be thou cast into the sea; and shall not doubt in his heart, but shall believe that those things which he saith shall come to pass; he shall have whatsoever he saith." – **Jesus, Mark 11:23***

Date Set:_____ Date Accomplished/Received:_____

**I Will BELIEVE the Unbelievable and RECEIVE the Impossible...
MY POWER IS IN MY SAYING AND BELIEVING!**

_____
_____
_____
_____
_____
_____
_____
_____
_____
_____
_____
_____
_____
_____
_____
_____
_____
_____
_____
_____
_____
_____
_____
_____
_____

*Date Set:*_____ *Date Accomplished/Received:*_____

*"For verily I say unto you, That whosoever shall say unto this mountain, Be thou removed, and be thou cast into the sea; and shall not doubt in his heart, but shall believe that those things which he saith shall come to pass; he shall have whatsoever he saith." – **Jesus, Mark 11:23***

Date Set:_____ Date Accomplished/Received:_____

**I Will BELIEVE the Unbelievable and RECEIVE the Impossible…
MY POWER IS IN MY SAYING AND BELIEVING!**

_____
_____
_____
_____
_____
_____
_____
_____
_____
_____
_____
_____
_____
_____
_____
_____
_____
_____
_____
_____
_____
_____
_____
_____
_____

Date Set:_____ Date Accomplished/Received:_____

*"For verily I say unto you, That whosoever shall say unto this mountain, Be thou removed, and be thou cast into the sea; and shall not doubt in his heart, but shall believe that those things which he saith shall come to pass; he shall have whatsoever he saith." – **Jesus, Mark 11:23**

_____
_____
_____
_____
_____
_____
_____
_____
_____
_____
_____
_____
_____
_____
_____
_____
_____
_____
_____
_____
_____
_____
_____
_____

*Date Set:*_____ *Date Accomplished/Received:*_____

**I Will BELIEVE the Unbelievable and RECEIVE the Impossible…
MY POWER IS IN MY SAYING AND BELIEVING!**

_____
_____
_____
_____
_____
_____
_____
_____
_____
_____
_____
_____
_____
_____
_____
_____
_____
_____
_____
_____
_____
_____
_____
_____

*Date Set:*_____ *Date Accomplished/Received:*_____

When you have a vision or a goal that you're working towards, never forget that you are not alone.

The reason "all things are possible" is because your goal has TWO forces working together to meet it—the wonderful mix of God *and* you. Break out of your old ways of thinking. Imagine! Have faith! Then, actively pursue what has been in your heart all along.

**I Will BELIEVE the Unbelievable and RECEIVE the Impossible…
MY POWER IS IN MY SAYING AND BELIEVING!**

_____
_____
_____
_____
_____
_____
_____
_____
_____
_____
_____
_____
_____
_____
_____
_____
_____
_____
_____
_____
_____
_____
_____
_____
_____

*Date Set:*_____ *Date Accomplished/Received:*_____

*"For verily I say unto you, That whosoever shall say unto this mountain, Be thou removed, and be thou cast into the sea; and shall not doubt in his heart, but shall believe that those things which he saith shall come to pass; he shall have whatsoever he saith." – **Jesus, Mark 11:23***

_____
_____
_____
_____
_____
_____
_____
_____
_____
_____
_____
_____
_____
_____
_____
_____
_____
_____
_____
_____
_____
_____
_____
_____
_____
_____
_____

Date Set:_____ Date Accomplished/Received:_____

**I Will BELIEVE the Unbelievable and RECEIVE the Impossible...
MY POWER IS IN MY SAYING AND BELIEVING!**

Date Set:_____ Date Accomplished/Received:_____

"For verily I say unto you, That whosoever shall say unto this mountain, Be thou removed, and be thou cast into the sea; and shall not doubt in his heart, but shall believe that those things which he saith shall come to pass; he shall have whatsoever he saith." – **Jesus, Mark 11:23**

_____
_____
_____
_____
_____
_____
_____
_____
_____
_____
_____
_____
_____
_____
_____
_____
_____
_____
_____
_____
_____
_____
_____
_____

*Date Set:*_____ *Date Accomplished/Received:*_____

**I Will BELIEVE the Unbelievable and RECEIVE the Impossible…
MY POWER IS IN MY SAYING AND BELIEVING!**

_____

_____

_____

_____

_____

_____

_____

_____

_____

_____

_____

_____

_____

_____

_____

_____

_____

_____

_____

_____

_____

_____

_____

_____

_____

_____

*Date Set:*_____ *Date Accomplished/Received:*_____

*"For verily I say unto you, That whosoever shall say unto this mountain, Be thou removed, and be thou cast into the sea; and shall not doubt in his heart, but shall believe that those things which he saith shall come to pass; he shall have whatsoever he saith." – **Jesus, Mark 11:23***

_____
_____
_____
_____
_____
_____
_____
_____
_____
_____
_____
_____
_____
_____
_____
_____
_____
_____
_____
_____
_____
_____
_____
_____
_____
_____
_____
_____

*Date Set:*_____ *Date Accomplished/Received:*_____

**I Will BELIEVE the Unbelievable and RECEIVE the Impossible…
MY POWER IS IN MY SAYING AND BELIEVING!**

_____

_____

_____

_____

_____

_____

_____

_____

_____

_____

_____

_____

_____

_____

_____

_____

_____

_____

_____

_____

_____

_____

_____

_____

*Date Set:*_____ *Date Accomplished/Received:*_____

*"For verily I say unto you, That whosoever shall say unto this mountain, Be thou removed, and be thou cast into the sea; and shall not doubt in his heart, but shall believe that those things which he saith shall come to pass; he shall have whatsoever he saith." – **Jesus, Mark 11:23**

_____
_____
_____
_____
_____
_____
_____
_____
_____
_____
_____
_____
_____
_____
_____
_____
_____
_____
_____
_____
_____
_____
_____
_____
_____

*Date Set:*_____ *Date Accomplished/Received:*_____

**I Will BELIEVE the Unbelievable and RECEIVE the Impossible…
MY POWER IS IN MY SAYING AND BELIEVING!**

_____
_____
_____
_____
_____
_____
_____
_____
_____
_____
_____
_____
_____
_____
_____
_____
_____
_____
_____
_____
_____
_____
_____

*Date Set:*_____ *Date Accomplished/Received:*_____

*"For verily I say unto you, That whosoever shall say unto this mountain, Be thou removed, and be thou cast into the sea; and shall not doubt in his heart, but shall believe that those things which he saith shall come to pass; he shall have whatsoever he saith." – **Jesus, Mark 11:23***

_____

_____

_____

_____

_____

_____

_____

_____

_____

_____

_____

_____

_____

_____

_____

_____

_____

_____

_____

_____

_____

_____

_____

_____

_____

*Date Set:*_____ *Date Accomplished/Received:*_____

**I Will BELIEVE the Unbelievable and RECEIVE the Impossible…
MY POWER IS IN MY SAYING AND BELIEVING!**

_Date Set:_____ _Date Accomplished/Received:_____

Studying the Word is what will help you to rightly divide the Word of truth so that what you apply works!

Your future is so important. Making a plan to study the Word is time well spent because what you learn from the Lord is critical to your well-being and to those you love. The more you take care of yourself (your mind and spirit), the more you will be able to pour out into the lives of others.

**I Will BELIEVE the Unbelievable and RECEIVE the Impossible…
MY POWER IS IN MY SAYING AND BELIEVING!**

_Date Set:_____ _Date Accomplished/Received:_____

"For verily I say unto you, That whosoever shall say unto this mountain, Be thou removed, and be thou cast into the sea; and shall not doubt in his heart, but shall believe that those things which he saith shall come to pass; he shall have whatsoever he saith." – **Jesus, Mark 11:23**

_____
_____
_____
_____
_____
_____
_____
_____
_____
_____
_____
_____
_____
_____
_____
_____
_____
_____
_____
_____
_____
_____
_____
_____

Date Set:_____ Date Accomplished/Received:_____

**I Will BELIEVE the Unbelievable and RECEIVE the Impossible…
MY POWER IS IN MY SAYING AND BELIEVING!**

_____
_____
_____
_____
_____
_____
_____
_____
_____
_____
_____
_____
_____
_____
_____
_____
_____
_____
_____
_____
_____
_____

*Date Set:*_____ *Date Accomplished/Received:*_____

"For verily I say unto you, That whosoever shall say unto this mountain, Be thou removed, and be thou cast into the sea; and shall not doubt in his heart, but shall believe that those things which he saith shall come to pass; he shall have whatsoever he saith." – **Jesus, Mark 11:23**

_____

_____

_____

_____

_____

_____

_____

_____

_____

_____

_____

_____

_____

_____

_____

_____

_____

_____

_____

_____

_____

_____

_____

_____

_____

_____

*Date Set:*_____ *Date Accomplished/Received:*_____

**I Will BELIEVE the Unbelievable and RECEIVE the Impossible...
MY POWER IS IN MY SAYING AND BELIEVING!**

_Date Set:_____ _Date Accomplished/Received:_____

"For verily I say unto you, That whosoever shall say unto this mountain, Be thou removed, and be thou cast into the sea; and shall not doubt in his heart, but shall believe that those things which he saith shall come to pass; he shall have whatsoever he saith." – **Jesus, Mark 11:23**

_____

_____

_____

_____

_____

_____

_____

_____

_____

_____

_____

_____

_____

_____

_____

_____

_____

_____

_____

_____

_____

_____

_____

*Date Set:*_____ *Date Accomplished/Received:*_____

**I Will BELIEVE the Unbelievable and RECEIVE the Impossible...
MY POWER IS IN MY SAYING AND BELIEVING!**

Date Set:_____ Date Accomplished/Received:_____

*"For verily I say unto you, That whosoever shall say unto this mountain, Be thou removed, and be thou cast into the sea; and shall not doubt in his heart, but shall believe that those things which he saith shall come to pass; he shall have whatsoever he saith." – **Jesus, Mark 11:23**

_____
_____
_____
_____
_____
_____
_____
_____
_____
_____
_____
_____
_____
_____
_____
_____
_____
_____
_____
_____
_____
_____
_____
_____
_____
_____
_____

*Date Set:*_____   *Date Accomplished/Received:*_____

I Will BELIEVE the Unbelievable and RECEIVE the Impossible...
MY POWER IS IN MY SAYING AND BELIEVING!

_____

_____

_____

_____

_____

_____

_____

_____

_____

_____

_____

_____

_____

_____

_____

_____

_____

_____

_____

_____

_____

_____

_____

_____

*Date Set:*_____ *Date Accomplished/Received:*_____

*"For verily I say unto you, That whosoever shall say unto this mountain, Be thou removed, and be thou cast into the sea; and shall not doubt in his heart, but shall believe that those things which he saith shall come to pass; he shall have whatsoever he saith." – **Jesus, Mark 11:23***

_____

_____

_____

_____

_____

_____

_____

_____

_____

_____

_____

_____

_____

_____

_____

_____

_____

_____

_____

_____

_____

_____

_____

*Date Set:*_____ *Date Accomplished/Received:*_____

**I Will BELIEVE the Unbelievable and RECEIVE the Impossible...
MY POWER IS IN MY SAYING AND BELIEVING!**

Date Set: _____ _Date Accomplished/Received:_ _____

I believe that God wants you to *let go*.

From the time you were born until now, you have absorbed many opinions about what you are capable of doing. What you believe you can and cannot do today is the culmination of what you've been told, what you've accepted, what you've told yourself, and what you assume to be true. In other words, it has nothing to do with what GOD says you can do. Therefore, all those inner thoughts about yourself are myths and fragments of old ideas and old fears of failure, and I believe God wants you to *let them go*. What will you replace them with? You will renew your mind with the Word. Forget what *they* said, what has God said about you?

**I Will BELIEVE the Unbelievable and RECEIVE the Impossible...
MY POWER IS IN MY SAYING AND BELIEVING!**

_____

_____

_____

_____

_____

_____

_____

_____

_____

_____

_____

_____

_____

_____

_____

_____

_____

_____

_____

_____

_____

_____

_____

*Date Set:*_____ *Date Accomplished/Received:*_____

*"For verily I say unto you, That whosoever shall say unto this mountain, Be thou removed, and be thou cast into the sea; and shall not doubt in his heart, but shall believe that those things which he saith shall come to pass; he shall have whatsoever he saith." – **Jesus, Mark 11:23***

_____

_____

_____

_____

_____

_____

_____

_____

_____

_____

_____

_____

_____

_____

_____

_____

_____

_____

_____

_____

_____

_____

_____

_____

_____

_____

*Date Set:*_____ *Date Accomplished/Received:*_____

**I Will BELIEVE the Unbelievable and RECEIVE the Impossible...
MY POWER IS IN MY SAYING AND BELIEVING!**

_____
_____
_____
_____
_____
_____
_____
_____
_____
_____
_____
_____
_____
_____
_____
_____
_____
_____
_____
_____
_____
_____
_____

*Date Set:*_____ *Date Accomplished/Received:*_____

*"For verily I say unto you, That whosoever shall say unto this mountain, Be thou removed, and be thou cast into the sea; and shall not doubt in his heart, but shall believe that those things which he saith shall come to pass; he shall have whatsoever he saith." – **Jesus, Mark 11:23***

_____
_____
_____
_____
_____
_____
_____
_____
_____
_____
_____
_____
_____
_____
_____
_____
_____
_____
_____
_____
_____
_____
_____
_____
_____
_____

*Date Set:*_____ *Date Accomplished/Received:*_____

**I Will BELIEVE the Unbelievable and RECEIVE the Impossible...
MY POWER IS IN MY SAYING AND BELIEVING!**

_____
_____
_____
_____
_____
_____
_____
_____
_____
_____
_____
_____
_____
_____
_____
_____
_____
_____
_____
_____
_____
_____
_____
_____

*Date Set:*_____ *Date Accomplished/Received:*_____

*"For verily I say unto you, That whosoever shall say unto this mountain, Be thou removed, and be thou cast into the sea; and shall not doubt in his heart, but shall believe that those things which he saith shall come to pass; he shall have whatsoever he saith." – **Jesus, Mark 11:23***

_____

_____

_____

_____

_____

_____

_____

_____

_____

_____

_____

_____

_____

_____

_____

_____

_____

_____

_____

_____

_____

_____

_____

_____

*Date Set:*_____   *Date Accomplished/Received:*_____

**I Will BELIEVE the Unbelievable and RECEIVE the Impossible…
MY POWER IS IN MY SAYING AND BELIEVING!**

_____

_____

_____

_____

_____

_____

_____

_____

_____

_____

_____

_____

_____

_____

_____

_____

_____

_____

_____

_____

_____

_____

_____

_____

_____

*Date Set:*_____ *Date Accomplished/Received:*_____

"For verily I say unto you, That whosoever shall say unto this mountain, Be thou removed, and be thou cast into the sea; and shall not doubt in his heart, but shall believe that those things which he saith shall come to pass; he shall have whatsoever he saith." – **Jesus, Mark 11:23**

Date Set:_____ Date Accomplished/Received:_____

**I Will BELIEVE the Unbelievable and RECEIVE the Impossible…
MY POWER IS IN MY SAYING AND BELIEVING!**

_Date Set:_____ _Date Accomplished/Received:_____

*"For verily I say unto you, That whosoever shall say unto this mountain, Be thou removed, and be thou cast into the sea; and shall not doubt in his heart, but shall believe that those things which he saith shall come to pass; he shall have whatsoever he saith." – **Jesus, Mark 11:23***

_____

_____

_____

_____

_____

_____

_____

_____

_____

_____

_____

_____

_____

_____

_____

_____

_____

_____

_____

_____

_____

_____

_____

_____

_____

_____

*Date Set:*_____ *Date Accomplished/Received:*_____

**I Will BELIEVE the Unbelievable and RECEIVE the Impossible…
MY POWER IS IN MY SAYING AND BELIEVING!**

*Date Set:*_____ *Date Accomplished/Received:*_____

God will never leave you or forsake you… but neither will He force you to reach those "unbelievable" and "impossible" needs, desires, and dreams that He has placed in your heart.

No, that is something you are going to have to do for yourself. It's time to create some FRICTION! It's time to forget what *they* may have said and FOCUS on what God says. It's time to put some FORCE behind the "unbelievable" and "impossible" things that have been percolating in your heart. What kind of force? The force of FAITH.

**I Will BELIEVE the Unbelievable and RECEIVE the Impossible…
MY POWER IS IN MY SAYING AND BELIEVING!**

Date Set:_____ Date Accomplished/Received:_____

*"For verily I say unto you, That whosoever shall say unto this mountain, Be thou removed, and be thou cast into the sea; and shall not doubt in his heart, but shall believe that those things which he saith shall come to pass; he shall have whatsoever he saith." – **Jesus, Mark 11:23***

*Date Set:*_____ *Date Accomplished/Received:*_____

**I Will BELIEVE the Unbelievable and RECEIVE the Impossible…
MY POWER IS IN MY SAYING AND BELIEVING!**

Date Set: _____ _Date Accomplished/Received:_ _____

*"For verily I say unto you, That whosoever shall say unto this mountain, Be thou removed, and be thou cast into the sea; and shall not doubt in his heart, but shall believe that those things which he saith shall come to pass; he shall have whatsoever he saith." – **Jesus, Mark 11:23***

Date Set:_____ Date Accomplished/Received:_____

**I Will BELIEVE the Unbelievable and RECEIVE the Impossible…
MY POWER IS IN MY SAYING AND BELIEVING!**

_Date Set:_____ _Date Accomplished/Received:_____

"For verily I say unto you, That whosoever shall say unto this mountain, Be thou removed, and be thou cast into the sea; and shall not doubt in his heart, but shall believe that those things which he saith shall come to pass; he shall have whatsoever he saith." – **Jesus, Mark 11:23**

_____

_____

_____

_____

_____

_____

_____

_____

_____

_____

_____

_____

_____

_____

_____

_____

_____

_____

_____

_____

_____

_____

_____

_____

_____

_____

Date Set:_____ Date Accomplished/Received:_____

I Will BELIEVE the Unbelievable and RECEIVE the Impossible...
MY POWER IS IN MY SAYING AND BELIEVING!

_____

_____

_____

_____

_____

_____

_____

_____

_____

_____

_____

_____

_____

_____

_____

_____

_____

_____

_____

_____

_____

_____

_____

*Date Set:*_____ *Date Accomplished/Received:*_____

"For verily I say unto you, That whosoever shall say unto this mountain, Be thou removed, and be thou cast into the sea; and shall not doubt in his heart, but shall believe that those things which he saith shall come to pass; he shall have whatsoever he saith." – **Jesus, Mark 11:23**

_____

_____

_____

_____

_____

_____

_____

_____

_____

_____

_____

_____

_____

_____

_____

_____

_____

_____

_____

_____

_____

_____

_____

_____

_____

_____

*Date Set:*_____ *Date Accomplished/Received:*_____

**I Will BELIEVE the Unbelievable and RECEIVE the Impossible...
MY POWER IS IN MY SAYING AND BELIEVING!**

_____
_____
_____
_____
_____
_____
_____
_____
_____
_____
_____
_____
_____
_____
_____
_____
_____
_____
_____
_____
_____
_____
_____

Date Set:_____ Date Accomplished/Received:_____

"For verily I say unto you, That whosoever shall say unto this mountain, Be thou removed, and be thou cast into the sea; and shall not doubt in his heart, but shall believe that those things which he saith shall come to pass; he shall have whatsoever he saith." – **Jesus, Mark 11:23**

_____
_____
_____
_____
_____
_____
_____
_____
_____
_____
_____
_____
_____
_____
_____
_____
_____
_____
_____
_____
_____
_____
_____
_____
_____
_____
_____

*Date Set:*_____ *Date Accomplished/Received:*_____

**I Will BELIEVE the Unbelievable and RECEIVE the Impossible...
MY POWER IS IN MY SAYING AND BELIEVING!**

_Date Set:_____ _Date Accomplished/Received:_____

Make your vision plain! Make it plain enough to read while you run through this race of life.

Remember, the Word wouldn't use those kinds of analogies if you weren't meant to DO what it says. Pray. Believe. Move forward. Forget what is behind and press forward to what is ahead. God has so much in store for you if you are willing to "only believe" and RUN your race!

**I Will BELIEVE the Unbelievable and RECEIVE the Impossible…
MY POWER IS IN MY SAYING AND BELIEVING!**

Date Set:_____ Date Accomplished/Received:_____

"For verily I say unto you, That whosoever shall say unto this mountain, Be thou removed, and be thou cast into the sea; and shall not doubt in his heart, but shall believe that those things which he saith shall come to pass; he shall have whatsoever he saith." – **Jesus, Mark 11:23**

_____

_____

_____

_____

_____

_____

_____

_____

_____

_____

_____

_____

_____

_____

_____

_____

_____

_____

_____

_____

_____

_____

_____

_____

_____

Date Set:_____ Date Accomplished/Received:_____

**I Will BELIEVE the Unbelievable and RECEIVE the Impossible…
MY POWER IS IN MY SAYING AND BELIEVING!**

_____

_____

_____

_____

_____

_____

_____

_____

_____

_____

_____

_____

_____

_____

_____

_____

_____

_____

_____

_____

_____

_____

_____

_____

_____

*Date Set:*_____ *Date Accomplished/Received:*_____

*"For verily I say unto you, That whosoever shall say unto this mountain, Be thou removed, and be thou cast into the sea; and shall not doubt in his heart, but shall believe that those things which he saith shall come to pass; he shall have whatsoever he saith." – **Jesus, Mark 11:23**

Date Set:_____ Date Accomplished/Received:_____

**I Will BELIEVE the Unbelievable and RECEIVE the Impossible...
MY POWER IS IN MY SAYING AND BELIEVING!**

_____
_____
_____
_____
_____
_____
_____
_____
_____
_____
_____
_____
_____
_____
_____
_____
_____
_____
_____
_____
_____
_____
_____
_____

Date Set:_____ Date Accomplished/Received:_____

*"For verily I say unto you, That whosoever shall say unto this mountain, Be thou removed, and be thou cast into the sea; and shall not doubt in his heart, but shall believe that those things which he saith shall come to pass; he shall have whatsoever he saith." – **Jesus, Mark 11:23**

Date Set:_____ Date Accomplished/Received:_____

**I Will BELIEVE the Unbelievable and RECEIVE the Impossible...
MY POWER IS IN MY SAYING AND BELIEVING!**

_____

_____

_____

_____

_____

_____

_____

_____

_____

_____

_____

_____

_____

_____

_____

_____

_____

_____

_____

_____

_____

*Date Set:*_____ *Date Accomplished/Received:*_____

"For verily I say unto you, That whosoever shall say unto this mountain, Be thou removed, and be thou cast into the sea; and shall not doubt in his heart, but shall believe that those things which he saith shall come to pass; he shall have whatsoever he saith." – **Jesus, Mark 11:23**

_____

_____

_____

_____

_____

_____

_____

_____

_____

_____

_____

_____

_____

_____

_____

_____

_____

_____

_____

_____

_____

_____

_____

_____

Date Set:_____ Date Accomplished/Received:_____

**I Will BELIEVE the Unbelievable and RECEIVE the Impossible…
MY POWER IS IN MY SAYING AND BELIEVING!**

_Date Set:_____ _Date Accomplished/Received:_____

*"For verily I say unto you, That whosoever shall say unto this mountain, Be thou removed, and be thou cast into the sea; and shall not doubt in his heart, but shall believe that those things which he saith shall come to pass; he shall have whatsoever he saith." – **Jesus, Mark 11:23***

Date Set:_____ Date Accomplished/Received:_____

**I Will BELIEVE the Unbelievable and RECEIVE the Impossible...
MY POWER IS IN MY SAYING AND BELIEVING!**

_____

_____

_____

_____

_____

_____

_____

_____

_____

_____

_____

_____

_____

_____

_____

_____

_____

_____

_____

_____

_____

_____

_____

*Date Set:*_____ *Date Accomplished/Received:*_____

If I'm not believing for the *un*believable, then I'm not believing!

After all, who in their right mind would tell a mountain to be removed and be thrown into the sea? I'll tell you who: You! Me! Believers like us around the world! We don't think with just the natural mind anymore because our eyes have been opened to the Spirit. Now we have faith in something beyond ourselves…in Someone Who is able to do exceedingly abundantly above all that we dare ask or think, according to the power that works in us (Ephesians 3:20).

The Word has changed my thinking, and now I know that if I'm not believing for the unbelievable, then I'm not really believing at all. God requires us to push ourselves and have faith because that's how we please Him. And besides, like Walt Disney said, "It's kind of fun to do the impossible!"

**I Will BELIEVE the Unbelievable and RECEIVE the Impossible…
MY POWER IS IN MY SAYING AND BELIEVING!**

_____

_____

_____

_____

_____

_____

_____

_____

_____

_____

_____

_____

_____

_____

_____

_____

_____

_____

_____

_____

_____

_____

_____

_____

*Date Set:*_____ *Date Accomplished/Received:*_____

*"For verily I say unto you, That whosoever shall say unto this mountain, Be thou removed, and be thou cast into the sea; and shall not doubt in his heart, but shall believe that those things which he saith shall come to pass; he shall have whatsoever he saith." – **Jesus, Mark 11:23**

Date Set:_____ Date Accomplished/Received:_____

**I Will BELIEVE the Unbelievable and RECEIVE the Impossible...
MY POWER IS IN MY SAYING AND BELIEVING!**

_____
_____
_____
_____
_____
_____
_____
_____
_____
_____
_____
_____
_____
_____
_____
_____
_____
_____
_____
_____
_____
_____

Date Set:_____ Date Accomplished/Received:_____

"For verily I say unto you, That whosoever shall say unto this mountain, Be thou removed, and be thou cast into the sea; and shall not doubt in his heart, but shall believe that those things which he saith shall come to pass; he shall have whatsoever he saith." – **Jesus, Mark 11:23**

_____
_____
_____
_____
_____
_____
_____
_____
_____
_____
_____
_____
_____
_____
_____
_____
_____
_____
_____
_____
_____
_____
_____
_____
_____

*Date Set:*_____ *Date Accomplished/Received:*_____

I Will BELIEVE the Unbelievable and RECEIVE the Impossible...
MY POWER IS IN MY SAYING AND BELIEVING!

Date Set:_____ Date Accomplished/Received:_____

*"For verily I say unto you, That whosoever shall say unto this mountain, Be thou removed, and be thou cast into the sea; and shall not doubt in his heart, but shall believe that those things which he saith shall come to pass; he shall have whatsoever he saith." – **Jesus, Mark 11:23**

_____
_____
_____
_____
_____
_____
_____
_____
_____
_____
_____
_____
_____
_____
_____
_____
_____
_____
_____
_____
_____
_____
_____
_____
_____
_____
_____

*Date Set:*_____ *Date Accomplished/Received:*_____

**I Will BELIEVE the Unbelievable and RECEIVE the Impossible…
MY POWER IS IN MY SAYING AND BELIEVING!**

_____
_____
_____
_____
_____
_____
_____
_____
_____
_____
_____
_____
_____
_____
_____
_____
_____
_____
_____
_____
_____
_____
_____
_____
_____
_____
_____

Date Set:_____   Date Accomplished/Received:_____

*"For verily I say unto you, That whosoever shall say unto this mountain, Be thou removed, and be thou cast into the sea; and shall not doubt in his heart, but shall believe that those things which he saith shall come to pass; he shall have whatsoever he saith." – **Jesus, Mark 11:23***

*Date Set:*_____ *Date Accomplished/Received:*_____

**I Will BELIEVE the Unbelievable and RECEIVE the Impossible...
MY POWER IS IN MY SAYING AND BELIEVING!**

_____

_____

_____

_____

_____

_____

_____

_____

_____

_____

_____

_____

_____

_____

_____

_____

_____

_____

_____

_____

_____

_____

*Date Set:*_____ *Date Accomplished/Received:*_____

"For verily I say unto you, That whosoever shall say unto this mountain, Be thou removed, and be thou cast into the sea; and shall not doubt in his heart, but shall believe that those things which he saith shall come to pass; he shall have whatsoever he saith." – **Jesus, Mark 11:23**

_____
_____
_____
_____
_____
_____
_____
_____
_____
_____
_____
_____
_____
_____
_____
_____
_____
_____
_____
_____
_____
_____
_____
_____
_____

*Date Set:*_____ *Date Accomplished/Received:*_____

**I Will BELIEVE the Unbelievable and RECEIVE the Impossible…
MY POWER IS IN MY SAYING AND BELIEVING!**

Date Set:_____ Date Accomplished/Received:_____

Your words are a key element to making things come to pass.

Remember, moving mountains requires words. Learn to "see it" and "say it" with conviction. Notice that Jesus told us to "say" something to the mountain. He stressed that it wasn't about words alone—He wants us to believe what we say and not doubt in our heart that what we are saying is indeed coming to pass. That means you've got to not only *say* something, but you've also got to *see* it in your spirit. Once you *see* it in your spirit, then nothing will stop it from happening if you continue to do what Jesus said. Say it. Believe it. Don't doubt it. See it inside first, and then you will see that "unbelievable" and "impossible" thing come to pass.

**I Will BELIEVE the Unbelievable and RECEIVE the Impossible…
MY POWER IS IN MY SAYING AND BELIEVING!**

_____
_____
_____
_____
_____
_____
_____
_____
_____
_____
_____
_____
_____
_____
_____
_____
_____
_____
_____
_____
_____
_____
_____
_____

*Date Set:*_____ *Date Accomplished/Received:*_____

"For verily I say unto you, That whosoever shall say unto this mountain, Be thou removed, and be thou cast into the sea; and shall not doubt in his heart, but shall believe that those things which he saith shall come to pass; he shall have whatsoever he saith." – **Jesus, Mark 11:23**

_____
_____
_____
_____
_____
_____
_____
_____
_____
_____
_____
_____
_____
_____
_____
_____
_____
_____
_____
_____
_____
_____

*Date Set:*_____ *Date Accomplished/Received:*_____

**I Will BELIEVE the Unbelievable and RECEIVE the Impossible...
MY POWER IS IN MY SAYING AND BELIEVING!**

_____

_____

_____

_____

_____

_____

_____

_____

_____

_____

_____

_____

_____

_____

_____

_____

_____

_____

_____

_____

_____

_____

_____

_____

Date Set:_____ Date Accomplished/Received:_____

"For verily I say unto you, That whosoever shall say unto this mountain, Be thou removed, and be thou cast into the sea; and shall not doubt in his heart, but shall believe that those things which he saith shall come to pass; he shall have whatsoever he saith." – **Jesus, Mark 11:23**

Date Set:_____ Date Accomplished/Received:_____

**I Will BELIEVE the Unbelievable and RECEIVE the Impossible…
MY POWER IS IN MY SAYING AND BELIEVING!**

_____
_____
_____
_____
_____
_____
_____
_____
_____
_____
_____
_____
_____
_____
_____
_____
_____
_____
_____
_____
_____
_____
_____
_____

Date Set:_____ Date Accomplished/Received:_____

*"For verily I say unto you, That whosoever shall say unto this mountain, Be thou removed, and be thou cast into the sea; and shall not doubt in his heart, but shall believe that those things which he saith shall come to pass; he shall have whatsoever he saith." – **Jesus, Mark 11:23**

Date Set:_____ Date Accomplished/Received:_____

**I Will BELIEVE the Unbelievable and RECEIVE the Impossible...
MY POWER IS IN MY SAYING AND BELIEVING!**

_____
_____
_____
_____
_____
_____
_____
_____
_____
_____
_____
_____
_____
_____
_____
_____
_____
_____
_____
_____
_____
_____
_____

Date Set:_____   Date Accomplished/Received:_____

*"For verily I say unto you, That whosoever shall say unto this mountain, Be thou removed, and be thou cast into the sea; and shall not doubt in his heart, but shall believe that those things which he saith shall come to pass; he shall have whatsoever he saith." – **Jesus, Mark 11:23***

Date Set:_____ Date Accomplished/Received:_____

**I Will BELIEVE the Unbelievable and RECEIVE the Impossible…
MY POWER IS IN MY SAYING AND BELIEVING!**

_____
_____
_____
_____
_____
_____
_____
_____
_____
_____
_____
_____
_____
_____
_____
_____
_____
_____
_____
_____
_____
_____
_____

*Date Set:*_____ *Date Accomplished/Received:*_____

*"For verily I say unto you, That whosoever shall say unto this mountain, Be thou removed, and be thou cast into the sea; and shall not doubt in his heart, but shall believe that those things which he saith shall come to pass; he shall have whatsoever he saith." – **Jesus, Mark 11:23***

Date Set:_____ Date Accomplished/Received:_____

**I Will BELIEVE the Unbelievable and RECEIVE the Impossible…
MY POWER IS IN MY SAYING AND BELIEVING!**

_____
_____
_____
_____
_____
_____
_____
_____
_____
_____
_____
_____
_____
_____
_____
_____
_____
_____
_____
_____
_____
_____

*Date Set:*_____ *Date Accomplished/Received:*_____

Don't let anything plug up your progress.

Just like in a stove or a heater, there is an igniter in your spirit to make it fire up and start giving you the desired result. In the Spirit, nothing should be allowed to plug up the igniting power of God's Word concerning your manifestation. What can plug up your progress? One thing: Doubt! **When you get to the place of** *"shall not doubt in his heart,"* **you are well on your way to having** *"whatsoever he saith."* Never forget that!

Check your heart, and not just your head. All of us get doubtful thoughts, but the Word says we are to bring every thought into captivity to the obedience of Christ, and that we're going to have to continue the process of putting down thoughts that rise up against what God has said (2 Corinthians 10:5).

How do you get doubt in your heart? It's a process. It happens when you don't put those doubtful thoughts down—when you allow those thoughts to stick around and you meditate on them so often that they find a home not only in your head, but also deep down in your heart. Banish them by renewing your mind (Romans 12:2). Keep them out by casting them down immediately when they rise up. Keep moving forward in faith!

**I Will BELIEVE the Unbelievable and RECEIVE the Impossible...
MY POWER IS IN MY SAYING AND BELIEVING!**

Date Set:_____ Date Accomplished/Received:_____

*"For verily I say unto you, That whosoever shall say unto this mountain, Be thou removed, and be thou cast into the sea; and shall not doubt in his heart, but shall believe that those things which he saith shall come to pass; he shall have whatsoever he saith." – **Jesus, Mark 11:23***

*Date Set:*_____ *Date Accomplished/Received:*_____

**I Will BELIEVE the Unbelievable and RECEIVE the Impossible...
MY POWER IS IN MY SAYING AND BELIEVING!**

_____
_____
_____
_____
_____
_____
_____
_____
_____
_____
_____
_____
_____
_____
_____
_____
_____
_____
_____
_____
_____
_____
_____
_____

*Date Set:*_____ *Date Accomplished/Received:*_____

*"For verily I say unto you, That whosoever shall say unto this mountain, Be thou removed, and be thou cast into the sea; and shall not doubt in his heart, but shall believe that those things which he saith shall come to pass; he shall have whatsoever he saith." – **Jesus, Mark 11:23**pan*

*Date Set:*_____ *Date Accomplished/Received:*_____

**I Will BELIEVE the Unbelievable and RECEIVE the Impossible...
MY POWER IS IN MY SAYING AND BELIEVING!**

_____
_____
_____
_____
_____
_____
_____
_____
_____
_____
_____
_____
_____
_____
_____
_____
_____
_____
_____
_____
_____
_____

*Date Set:*_____ *Date Accomplished/Received:*_____

"For verily I say unto you, That whosoever shall say unto this mountain, Be thou removed, and be thou cast into the sea; and shall not doubt in his heart, but shall believe that those things which he saith shall come to pass; he shall have whatsoever he saith." – **Jesus, Mark 11:23**

_____

_____

_____

_____

_____

_____

_____

_____

_____

_____

_____

_____

_____

_____

_____

_____

_____

_____

_____

_____

_____

_____

_____

_____

_____

Date Set:_____ Date Accomplished/Received:_____

**I Will BELIEVE the Unbelievable and RECEIVE the Impossible…
MY POWER IS IN MY SAYING AND BELIEVING!**

_____
_____
_____
_____
_____
_____
_____
_____
_____
_____
_____
_____
_____
_____
_____
_____
_____
_____
_____
_____
_____
_____

*Date Set:*_____ *Date Accomplished/Received:*_____

"For verily I say unto you, That whosoever shall say unto this mountain, Be thou removed, and be thou cast into the sea; and shall not doubt in his heart, but shall believe that those things which he saith shall come to pass; he shall have whatsoever he saith." – **Jesus, Mark 11:23**

_____
_____
_____
_____
_____
_____
_____
_____
_____
_____
_____
_____
_____
_____
_____
_____
_____
_____
_____
_____
_____
_____
_____
_____
_____

*Date Set:*_____ *Date Accomplished/Received:*_____

**I Will BELIEVE the Unbelievable and RECEIVE the Impossible...
MY POWER IS IN MY SAYING AND BELIEVING!**

_____
_____
_____
_____
_____
_____
_____
_____
_____
_____
_____
_____
_____
_____
_____
_____
_____
_____
_____
_____
_____
_____
_____
_____
_____

*Date Set:*_____ *Date Accomplished/Received:*_____

*"For verily I say unto you, That whosoever shall say unto this mountain, Be thou removed, and be thou cast into the sea; and shall not doubt in his heart, but shall believe that those things which he saith shall come to pass; he shall have whatsoever he saith." – **Jesus, Mark 11:23***

_____
_____
_____
_____
_____
_____
_____
_____
_____
_____
_____
_____
_____
_____
_____
_____
_____
_____
_____
_____
_____
_____
_____
_____

*Date Set:*_____ *Date Accomplished/Received:*_____

**I Will BELIEVE the Unbelievable and RECEIVE the Impossible…
MY POWER IS IN MY SAYING AND BELIEVING!**

_____
_____
_____
_____
_____
_____
_____
_____
_____
_____
_____
_____
_____
_____
_____
_____
_____
_____
_____
_____
_____
_____
_____
_____

*Date Set:*_____ *Date Accomplished/Received:*_____

Our faith is based on Christ and Him crucified and on the holy Word of God, which is the only real Truth that there is in this world.

Jesus said, *"I am the Way, the Truth and the Life: no man cometh to the Father, but by Me"* (John 14:6). So, we don't just read the Words of our Mediator, Jesus Christ, but we also endeavor to follow His ways—and His way is for us to say to the mountain, not doubt in our heart, and to believe that we will have whatever it is that we say.

Say what you want, not what you have. Speak the future into the present. It's what Jesus said to do. You can get His Word and His way of doing things in your heart to such a degree that nobody will be able to change your mind about what you're saying…even if it *is* unbelievable and impossible! It's all faith anyway, so why not put it towards what really matters to you? Say what you want!

**I Will BELIEVE the Unbelievable and RECEIVE the Impossible…
MY POWER IS IN MY SAYING AND BELIEVING!**

_____

_____

_____

_____

_____

_____

_____

_____

_____

_____

_____

_____

_____

_____

_____

_____

_____

_____

_____

_____

_____

_____

_____

*Date Set:*_____ *Date Accomplished/Received:*_____

*"For verily I say unto you, That whosoever shall say unto this mountain, Be thou removed, and be thou cast into the sea; and shall not doubt in his heart, but shall believe that those things which he saith shall come to pass; he shall have whatsoever he saith." – **Jesus, Mark 11:23***

_____

_____

_____

_____

_____

_____

_____

_____

_____

_____

_____

_____

_____

_____

_____

_____

_____

_____

_____

_____

_____

_____

_____

*Date Set:*_____ *Date Accomplished/Received:*_____

I Will BELIEVE the Unbelievable and RECEIVE the Impossible…
MY POWER IS IN MY SAYING AND BELIEVING!

_Date Set:_____ _Date Accomplished/Received:_____

*"For verily I say unto you, That whosoever shall say unto this mountain, Be thou removed, and be thou cast into the sea; and shall not doubt in his heart, but shall believe that those things which he saith shall come to pass; he shall have whatsoever he saith." – **Jesus, Mark 11:23***

Date Set:_____ Date Accomplished/Received:_____

**I Will BELIEVE the Unbelievable and RECEIVE the Impossible…
MY POWER IS IN MY SAYING AND BELIEVING!**

_Date Set:_____ _Date Accomplished/Received:_____

*"For verily I say unto you, That whosoever shall say unto this mountain, Be thou removed, and be thou cast into the sea; and shall not doubt in his heart, but shall believe that those things which he saith shall come to pass; he shall have whatsoever he saith." – **Jesus, Mark 11:23***

_____
_____
_____
_____
_____
_____
_____
_____
_____
_____
_____
_____
_____
_____
_____
_____
_____
_____
_____
_____
_____
_____
_____

Date Set:_____ Date Accomplished/Received:_____

**I Will BELIEVE the Unbelievable and RECEIVE the Impossible…
MY POWER IS IN MY SAYING AND BELIEVING!**

_____
_____
_____
_____
_____
_____
_____
_____
_____
_____
_____
_____
_____
_____
_____
_____
_____
_____
_____
_____
_____
_____

*Date Set:*_____ *Date Accomplished/Received:*_____

"For verily I say unto you, That whosoever shall say unto this mountain, Be thou removed, and be thou cast into the sea; and shall not doubt in his heart, but shall believe that those things which he saith shall come to pass; he shall have whatsoever he saith." – **Jesus, Mark 11:23**

_____

_____

_____

_____

_____

_____

_____

_____

_____

_____

_____

_____

_____

_____

_____

_____

_____

_____

_____

_____

_____

_____

_____

_____

_____

_____

*Date Set:*_____ *Date Accomplished/Received:*_____

I Will BELIEVE the Unbelievable and RECEIVE the Impossible...
MY POWER IS IN MY SAYING AND BELIEVING!

_____

_____

_____

_____

_____

_____

_____

_____

_____

_____

_____

_____

_____

_____

_____

_____

_____

_____

_____

_____

_____

_____

*Date Set:*_____ *Date Accomplished/Received:*_____

*"For verily I say unto you, That whosoever shall say unto this mountain, Be thou removed, and be thou cast into the sea; and shall not doubt in his heart, but shall believe that those things which he saith shall come to pass; he shall have whatsoever he saith." – **Jesus, Mark 11:23***

_____
_____
_____
_____
_____
_____
_____
_____
_____
_____
_____
_____
_____
_____
_____
_____
_____
_____
_____
_____
_____
_____
_____
_____
_____

*Date Set:*_____ *Date Accomplished/Received:*_____

**I Will BELIEVE the Unbelievable and RECEIVE the Impossible…
MY POWER IS IN MY SAYING AND BELIEVING!**

_____
_____
_____
_____
_____
_____
_____
_____
_____
_____
_____
_____
_____
_____
_____
_____
_____
_____
_____
_____
_____
_____

*Date Set:*_____ *Date Accomplished/Received:*_____

If the Word says you can have it, then it's a done deal.

One of the greatest insights about God in the Word is found in Numbers 23:19, *"God is not a man, that He should lie; neither the son of man, that He should repent: hath He said, and shall He not do it? Or hath He spoken, and shall He not make it good?"* God can't lie! His Word says you can be out of debt. That's "unbelievable" in this day and age. His Word says that you can be healed. That's "impossible" in any age. His Word says that you can love your enemies. That's both unbelievable and impossible! Do you see where I'm going? It's time to realize that if God said it, then it is true. He specializes in the unbelievable and the impossible. For those who believe, the future is exciting! Listen closely. Can you hear the shouts of joy in your future? They are coming…they are on their way…I'm prophesying it right now. Glory!

**I Will BELIEVE the Unbelievable and RECEIVE the Impossible…
MY POWER IS IN MY SAYING AND BELIEVING!**

_____
_____
_____
_____
_____
_____
_____
_____
_____
_____
_____
_____
_____
_____
_____
_____
_____
_____
_____
_____
_____
_____
_____

*Date Set:*_____ *Date Accomplished/Received:*_____

"For verily I say unto you, That whosoever shall say unto this mountain, Be thou removed, and be thou cast into the sea; and shall not doubt in his heart, but shall believe that those things which he saith shall come to pass; he shall have whatsoever he saith." – **Jesus, Mark 11:23**

Date Set:_____ Date Accomplished/Received:_____

**I Will BELIEVE the Unbelievable and RECEIVE the Impossible…
MY POWER IS IN MY SAYING AND BELIEVING!**

_____

_____

_____

_____

_____

_____

_____

_____

_____

_____

_____

_____

_____

_____

_____

_____

_____

_____

_____

_____

_____

_____

_____

_____

_____

*Date Set:*_____ *Date Accomplished/Received:*_____

*"For verily I say unto you, That whosoever shall say unto this mountain, Be thou removed, and be thou cast into the sea; and shall not doubt in his heart, but shall believe that those things which he saith shall come to pass; he shall have whatsoever he saith." – **Jesus, Mark 11:23**

Date Set:_____ Date Accomplished/Received:_____

**I Will BELIEVE the Unbelievable and RECEIVE the Impossible...
MY POWER IS IN MY SAYING AND BELIEVING!**

_Date Set:_____ _Date Accomplished/Received:_____

*"For verily I say unto you, That whosoever shall say unto this mountain, Be thou removed, and be thou cast into the sea; and shall not doubt in his heart, but shall believe that those things which he saith shall come to pass; he shall have whatsoever he saith." – **Jesus, Mark 11:23**__

Date Set:_____ Date Accomplished/Received:_____

**I Will BELIEVE the Unbelievable and RECEIVE the Impossible...
MY POWER IS IN MY SAYING AND BELIEVING!**

_Date Set:_____ _Date Accomplished/Received:_____

*"For verily I say unto you, That whosoever shall say unto this mountain, Be thou removed, and be thou cast into the sea; and shall not doubt in his heart, but shall believe that those things which he saith shall come to pass; he shall have whatsoever he saith." – **Jesus, Mark 11:23**

Date Set:_____ Date Accomplished/Received:_____

**I Will BELIEVE the Unbelievable and RECEIVE the Impossible…
MY POWER IS IN MY SAYING AND BELIEVING!**

Date Set:_____ Date Accomplished/Received:_____

"For verily I say unto you, That whosoever shall say unto this mountain, Be thou removed, and be thou cast into the sea; and shall not doubt in his heart, but shall believe that those things which he saith shall come to pass; he shall have whatsoever he saith." – *Jesus, Mark 11:23*

_____
_____
_____
_____
_____
_____
_____
_____
_____
_____
_____
_____
_____
_____
_____
_____
_____
_____
_____
_____
_____
_____
_____
_____
_____

*Date Set:*_____ *Date Accomplished/Received:*_____

I Will BELIEVE the Unbelievable and RECEIVE the Impossible...
MY POWER IS IN MY SAYING AND BELIEVING!

_____
_____
_____
_____
_____
_____
_____
_____
_____
_____
_____
_____
_____
_____
_____
_____
_____
_____
_____
_____
_____
_____
_____

*Date Set:*_____ *Date Accomplished/Received:*_____

Don't overlook what needs to be *made* right.

Put a spotlight on your life to see if you've overlooked something that needs to be made right. In the past, when I've questioned why something wasn't working, I've found that stopping and assessing myself—putting a spotlight on my own life—showed that I had overlooked something that needed correcting. Sometimes it was a small thing and other times it was something I'd nearly forgotten, but each time it was something I needed to make right so that my prayers would work more effectively.

There is only one "spotlight" that is acceptable: the Holy Spirit. You can trust the Holy Spirit! He will reveal things to you that you need to correct. He will never lead you on a wrong path, and He will always walk in truth. John 16:13-15 says, *"Howbeit when He, the Spirit of truth, is come, He will guide you into all truth: for He shall not speak of Himself; but whatsoever He shall hear, that shall He speak: and He will shew you things to come. He shall glorify Me: for He shall receive of Mine, and shall shew it unto you. All things that the Father hath are Mine: therefore said I, that He shall take of Mine, and shall shew it unto you."*

When you pray, ask the Holy Spirit to reveal anything about yourself that is blocking your way in life. I promise that if you are honest with yourself and allow Him to speak to you, He will show you what you need to do to make things right. And, when you obey His prompting and do it—whether it is forgiving someone, going back and saying something you should have said, doing something you should have done, apologizing, giving, helping… whatever it is—I promise that the act of obedience itself will open your life back up to the blessings the scriptures offer to those who believe.

**I Will BELIEVE the Unbelievable and RECEIVE the Impossible...
MY POWER IS IN MY SAYING AND BELIEVING!**

_____

_____

_____

_____

_____

_____

_____

_____

_____

_____

_____

_____

_____

_____

_____

_____

_____

_____

_____

_____

*Date Set:*_____ *Date Accomplished/Received:*_____

*"For verily I say unto you, That whosoever shall say unto this mountain, Be thou removed, and be thou cast into the sea; and shall not doubt in his heart, but shall believe that those things which he saith shall come to pass; he shall have whatsoever he saith." – **Jesus, Mark 11:23***

_____
_____
_____
_____
_____
_____
_____
_____
_____
_____
_____
_____
_____
_____
_____
_____
_____
_____
_____
_____
_____
_____
_____

Date Set:_____ Date Accomplished/Received:_____

**I Will BELIEVE the Unbelievable and RECEIVE the Impossible...
MY POWER IS IN MY SAYING AND BELIEVING!**

_____
_____
_____
_____
_____
_____
_____
_____
_____
_____
_____
_____
_____
_____
_____
_____
_____
_____
_____
_____
_____
_____

*Date Set:*_____ *Date Accomplished/Received:*_____

*"For verily I say unto you, That whosoever shall say unto this mountain, Be thou removed, and be thou cast into the sea; and shall not doubt in his heart, but shall believe that those things which he saith shall come to pass; he shall have whatsoever he saith." – **Jesus, Mark 11:23***

_____
_____
_____
_____
_____
_____
_____
_____
_____
_____
_____
_____
_____
_____
_____
_____
_____
_____
_____
_____
_____
_____
_____
_____
_____
_____
_____

*Date Set:*_____ *Date Accomplished/Received:*_____

**I Will BELIEVE the Unbelievable and RECEIVE the Impossible...
MY POWER IS IN MY SAYING AND BELIEVING!**

_____
_____
_____
_____
_____
_____
_____
_____
_____
_____
_____
_____
_____
_____
_____
_____
_____
_____
_____
_____
_____
_____

*Date Set:*_____ *Date Accomplished/Received:*_____

"For verily I say unto you, That whosoever shall say unto this mountain, Be thou removed, and be thou cast into the sea; and shall not doubt in his heart, but shall believe that those things which he saith shall come to pass; he shall have whatsoever he saith." – **Jesus, Mark 11:23**

_____
_____
_____
_____
_____
_____
_____
_____
_____
_____
_____
_____
_____
_____
_____
_____
_____
_____
_____
_____
_____
_____
_____
_____
_____

*Date Set:*_____ *Date Accomplished/Received:*_____

I Will BELIEVE the Unbelievable and RECEIVE the Impossible...
MY POWER IS IN MY SAYING AND BELIEVING!

_____

_____

_____

_____

_____

_____

_____

_____

_____

_____

_____

_____

_____

_____

_____

_____

_____

_____

_____

_____

_____

_____

_____

_____

_____

*Date Set:*_____ *Date Accomplished/Received:*_____

*"For verily I say unto you, That whosoever shall say unto this mountain, Be thou removed, and be thou cast into the sea; and shall not doubt in his heart, but shall believe that those things which he saith shall come to pass; he shall have whatsoever he saith." – **Jesus, Mark 11:23***

*Date Set:*_____ *Date Accomplished/Received:*_____

**I Will BELIEVE the Unbelievable and RECEIVE the Impossible…
MY POWER IS IN MY SAYING AND BELIEVING!**

_____
_____
_____
_____
_____
_____
_____
_____
_____
_____
_____
_____
_____
_____
_____
_____
_____
_____
_____
_____
_____
_____
_____
_____

*Date Set:*_____ *Date Accomplished/Received:*_____

"For verily I say unto you, That whosoever shall say unto this mountain, Be thou removed, and be thou cast into the sea; and shall not doubt in his heart, but shall believe that those things which he saith shall come to pass; he shall have whatsoever he saith." – **Jesus, Mark 11:23**

_____

_____

_____

_____

_____

_____

_____

_____

_____

_____

_____

_____

_____

_____

_____

_____

_____

_____

_____

_____

_____

_____

_____

_____

*Date Set:*_____ *Date Accomplished/Received:*_____

**I Will BELIEVE the Unbelievable and RECEIVE the Impossible…
MY POWER IS IN MY SAYING AND BELIEVING!**

_____
_____
_____
_____
_____
_____
_____
_____
_____
_____
_____
_____
_____
_____
_____
_____
_____
_____
_____
_____
_____
_____

*Date Set:*_____ *Date Accomplished/Received:*_____

God desires your success—spiritually, physically, financially, and in every way.

There are probably so many things you want in this life, and you should have them—God put some wonderful desires in you and He wants you to believe Him for whatever is on your heart. God is a good Father and He wants the best for every one of His children. Just as He doesn't want any of us to perish but have everlasting life, He also wants all of us to have peace, to live with joy, to be healthy, to prosper, and to realize our potential in this life…all while we're helping others and establishing His covenant on the earth. The Word is full of God's GOOD thoughts toward us. I know that the Church doesn't believe and teach that, but God does believe it and His Word does teach it! I will not let any religious denomination limit what God has for you or for me—His Word is FULL of the unbelievable and the impossible. We CAN do this! With God, nothing is impossible! If He is for us, who can be against us?

**I Will BELIEVE the Unbelievable and RECEIVE the Impossible…
MY POWER IS IN MY SAYING AND BELIEVING!**

Date Set:_____ Date Accomplished/Received:_____

*"For verily I say unto you, That whosoever shall say unto this mountain, Be thou removed, and be thou cast into the sea; and shall not doubt in his heart, but shall believe that those things which he saith shall come to pass; he shall have whatsoever he saith." – **Jesus, Mark 11:23**

_____
_____
_____
_____
_____
_____
_____
_____
_____
_____
_____
_____
_____
_____
_____
_____
_____
_____
_____
_____
_____
_____
_____
_____
_____
_____

*Date Set:*_____ *Date Accomplished/Received:*_____

**I Will BELIEVE the Unbelievable and RECEIVE the Impossible…
MY POWER IS IN MY SAYING AND BELIEVING!**

Date Set: _____ _Date Accomplished/Received:_ _____

*"For verily I say unto you, That whosoever shall say unto this mountain, Be thou removed, and be thou cast into the sea; and shall not doubt in his heart, but shall believe that those things which he saith shall come to pass; he shall have whatsoever he saith." – **Jesus, Mark 11:23***

_____
_____
_____
_____
_____
_____
_____
_____
_____
_____
_____
_____
_____
_____
_____
_____
_____
_____
_____
_____
_____
_____
_____
_____

*Date Set:*_____ *Date Accomplished/Received:*_____

**I Will BELIEVE the Unbelievable and RECEIVE the Impossible…
MY POWER IS IN MY SAYING AND BELIEVING!**

Date Set:_____ Date Accomplished/Received:_____

*"For verily I say unto you, That whosoever shall say unto this mountain, Be thou removed, and be thou cast into the sea; and shall not doubt in his heart, but shall believe that those things which he saith shall come to pass; he shall have whatsoever he saith." – **Jesus, Mark 11:23**

_____
_____
_____
_____
_____
_____
_____
_____
_____
_____
_____
_____
_____
_____
_____
_____
_____
_____
_____
_____
_____
_____
_____
_____
_____

*Date Set:*_____ *Date Accomplished/Received:*_____

**I Will BELIEVE the Unbelievable and RECEIVE the Impossible…
MY POWER IS IN MY SAYING AND BELIEVING!**

_____
_____
_____
_____
_____
_____
_____
_____
_____
_____
_____
_____
_____
_____
_____
_____
_____
_____
_____
_____
_____
_____
_____

*Date Set:*_____ *Date Accomplished/Received:*_____

*"For verily I say unto you, That whosoever shall say unto this mountain, Be thou removed, and be thou cast into the sea; and shall not doubt in his heart, but shall believe that those things which he saith shall come to pass; he shall have whatsoever he saith." – **Jesus, Mark 11:23***

_____

_____

_____

_____

_____

_____

_____

_____

_____

_____

_____

_____

_____

_____

_____

_____

_____

_____

_____

_____

_____

_____

_____

_____

_____

*Date Set:*_____ *Date Accomplished/Received:*_____

**I Will BELIEVE the Unbelievable and RECEIVE the Impossible…
MY POWER IS IN MY SAYING AND BELIEVING!**

Date Set:_____ Date Accomplished/Received:_____

*"For verily I say unto you, That whosoever shall say unto this mountain, Be thou removed, and be thou cast into the sea; and shall not doubt in his heart, but shall believe that those things which he saith shall come to pass; he shall have whatsoever he saith." – **Jesus, Mark 11:23***

_____
_____
_____
_____
_____
_____
_____
_____
_____
_____
_____
_____
_____
_____
_____
_____
_____
_____
_____
_____
_____
_____
_____
_____
_____

*Date Set:*_____ *Date Accomplished/Received:*_____

**I Will BELIEVE the Unbelievable and RECEIVE the Impossible…
MY POWER IS IN MY SAYING AND BELIEVING!**

_____
_____
_____
_____
_____
_____
_____
_____
_____
_____
_____
_____
_____
_____
_____
_____
_____
_____
_____
_____
_____
_____
_____
_____

*Date Set:*_____ *Date Accomplished/Received:*_____

One of the worst hindrances that will stop the Word from working in your life is STRIFE!

"And when ye stand praying, forgive, if ye have ought against any: that your Father also which is in Heaven may forgive you your trespasses. But if ye do not forgive, neither will your Father which is in Heaven forgive your trespasses" (Mark 11:25-26). So, if you want God's Word to "work" for you, then make sure there is no strife anywhere or against anyone in your life. This is so important. I've had a lot of people hurt me in my life, but I chose not to walk in strife. You see, I always knew it was my choice. If I was going to "believe the unbelievable and receive the impossible," then I had to crucify my flesh. I certainly didn't want to hinder myself. I knew God's Word was true, so I made the choice not to become what I hate—and that is a person of strife!

Forgiveness is a pathway to power. No matter who comes against you, no matter who hurts you (even if they "despitefully use you" as Jesus warned some people would do to you), make a quality choice now not to allow those attacks to rob you of your future. If you allow the devil to string you along with inner strife, you will give up the divine power of being a forgiver who is "right" with God.

You see, you can be saved and do wonderful things for God and other people and yet still remain in a powerless mode because of the inner strife of unforgiveness. If you pray all day long about something and never see it come to pass the way it should, check your heart.

Remember, just as Jesus promised you that you could have "whatsoever you saith" when you do things as He said, Jesus also promised that His Father would NOT forgive *you* until you forgive others. It works both ways. And that is why so many people have found that there is true power in forgiveness. So, what does it mean to your relationship with God if you maintain inner strife? It means that no matter what you do, you are not "right" with the Lord. There is something standing in the way of Him forgiving you. There is something standing in the way of you having access to His divine power.

You see, you just can't "believe the unbelievable and receive the impossible" on your own. Christ's teaching is not a mind over matter message; it's a divine principle. It requires connection to God. The bottom line? You need God's *power* working in your life to see God's *Word* come to pass.

**I Will BELIEVE the Unbelievable and RECEIVE the Impossible...
MY POWER IS IN MY SAYING AND BELIEVING!**

_____

_____

_____

_____

_____

_____

_____

_____

_____

_____

_____

_____

_____

_____

_____

_____

_____

_____

_____

_____

*Date Set:*_____ *Date Accomplished/Received:*_____

*"For verily I say unto you, That whosoever shall say unto this mountain, Be thou removed, and be thou cast into the sea; and shall not doubt in his heart, but shall believe that those things which he saith shall come to pass; he shall have whatsoever he saith." – **Jesus, Mark 11:23***

_____

_____

_____

_____

_____

_____

_____

_____

_____

_____

_____

_____

_____

_____

_____

_____

_____

_____

_____

_____

_____

_____

_____

_____

_____

_____

*Date Set:*_____ *Date Accomplished/Received:*_____

**I Will BELIEVE the Unbelievable and RECEIVE the Impossible...
MY POWER IS IN MY SAYING AND BELIEVING!**

Date Set: _____ _Date Accomplished/Received:_ _____

*"For verily I say unto you, That whosoever shall say unto this mountain, Be thou removed, and be thou cast into the sea; and shall not doubt in his heart, but shall believe that those things which he saith shall come to pass; he shall have whatsoever he saith." – **Jesus, Mark 11:23***

Date Set:_____ Date Accomplished/Received:_____

**I Will BELIEVE the Unbelievable and RECEIVE the Impossible…
MY POWER IS IN MY SAYING AND BELIEVING!**

_Date Set:_____ _Date Accomplished/Received:_____

*"For verily I say unto you, That whosoever shall say unto this mountain, Be thou removed, and be thou cast into the sea; and shall not doubt in his heart, but shall believe that those things which he saith shall come to pass; he shall have whatsoever he saith." – **Jesus, Mark 11:23***

_____
_____
_____
_____
_____
_____
_____
_____
_____
_____
_____
_____
_____
_____
_____
_____
_____
_____
_____
_____
_____
_____
_____

*Date Set:*_____ *Date Accomplished/Received:*_____

**I Will BELIEVE the Unbelievable and RECEIVE the Impossible...
MY POWER IS IN MY SAYING AND BELIEVING!**

_____
_____
_____
_____
_____
_____
_____
_____
_____
_____
_____
_____
_____
_____
_____
_____
_____
_____
_____
_____
_____
_____
_____
_____

*Date Set:*_____ *Date Accomplished/Received:*_____

*"For verily I say unto you, That whosoever shall say unto this mountain, Be thou removed, and be thou cast into the sea; and shall not doubt in his heart, but shall believe that those things which he saith shall come to pass; he shall have whatsoever he saith." – **Jesus, Mark 11:23**

_____
_____
_____
_____
_____
_____
_____
_____
_____
_____
_____
_____
_____
_____
_____
_____
_____
_____
_____
_____
_____
_____
_____
_____
_____

*Date Set:*_____ *Date Accomplished/Received:*_____

**I Will BELIEVE the Unbelievable and RECEIVE the Impossible…
MY POWER IS IN MY SAYING AND BELIEVING!**

_____
_____
_____
_____
_____
_____
_____
_____
_____
_____
_____
_____
_____
_____
_____
_____
_____
_____
_____
_____
_____
_____
_____

*Date Set:*_____ *Date Accomplished/Received:*_____

*"For verily I say unto you, That whosoever shall say unto this mountain, Be thou removed, and be thou cast into the sea; and shall not doubt in his heart, but shall believe that those things which he saith shall come to pass; he shall have whatsoever he saith." – **Jesus, Mark 11:23***

_____
_____
_____
_____
_____
_____
_____
_____
_____
_____
_____
_____
_____
_____
_____
_____
_____
_____
_____
_____
_____
_____
_____
_____
_____

*Date Set:*_____ *Date Accomplished/Received:*_____

**I Will BELIEVE the Unbelievable and RECEIVE the Impossible…
MY POWER IS IN MY SAYING AND BELIEVING!**

_____

_____

_____

_____

_____

_____

_____

_____

_____

_____

_____

_____

_____

_____

_____

_____

_____

_____

_____

_____

_____

_____

_____

*Date Set:*_____ *Date Accomplished/Received:*_____

The right words are always God's Words.

If you want to move mountainous problems out of your view… if you want to have whatsoever you say when you pray…if you want the desires of your heart to be met by making your words line up properly with God's Word...then not only must you relinquish strife, but you must also concentrate on what is coming out of your mouth.

Jesus told us in Matthew 12:34-37 that our words matter when He said, *"…for out of the abundance of the heart the mouth speaketh. A good man out of the good treasure of the heart bringeth forth good things: and an evil man out of the evil treasure bringeth forth evil things. But I say unto you, That every idle word that men shall speak, they shall give account thereof in the day of judgment. For by thy words thou shalt be justified, and by thy words thou shalt be condemned."*

This "unbelievable" principle that Jesus taught means that your words hold your destiny. They help you believe the unbelievable and receive the impossible! So, if by our words we are justified and by our words we are condemned, then our words have the power to either make us or break us. This is why Jesus focused on speaking to the mountain in Matthew 11:23. Notice that He used the words *"Whosoever shall say"* (not just pray) when He was talking about moving mountains in life.

You see, when you pray, you are usually asking *God* to do something. Jesus told us that in addition to prayer, we should also use the power of words. If we are right with God, then we are in connection with His power and so our words, like His words, also have power.

Your words hold your destiny. They can help you to believe what seems unbelievable to you. They can help you receive what seems impossible to you. This is not only the power of right standing with God, but also the power of faith and the words of your mouth.

Always say what the Word says. Now, it may seem unbelievable and impossible to you, but remember that *Jesus* said you could do and have these things—and He was sinless, blameless, and He did not lie. Glory!

**I Will BELIEVE the Unbelievable and RECEIVE the Impossible…
MY POWER IS IN MY SAYING AND BELIEVING!**

_____

_____

_____

_____

_____

_____

_____

_____

_____

_____

_____

_____

_____

_____

_____

_____

_____

_____

_____

_____

*Date Set:*_____ *Date Accomplished/Received:*_____

*"For verily I say unto you, That whosoever shall say unto this mountain, Be thou removed, and be thou cast into the sea; and shall not doubt in his heart, but shall believe that those things which he saith shall come to pass; he shall have whatsoever he saith." – **Jesus, Mark 11:23**

_____
_____
_____
_____
_____
_____
_____
_____
_____
_____
_____
_____
_____
_____
_____
_____
_____
_____
_____
_____
_____
_____
_____
_____

*Date Set:*_____ *Date Accomplished/Received:*_____

**I Will BELIEVE the Unbelievable and RECEIVE the Impossible...
MY POWER IS IN MY SAYING AND BELIEVING!**

_____

_____

_____

_____

_____

_____

_____

_____

_____

_____

_____

_____

_____

_____

_____

_____

_____

_____

_____

_____

_____

_____

_____

_____

*Date Set:*_____ *Date Accomplished/Received:*_____

*"For verily I say unto you, That whosoever shall say unto this mountain, Be thou removed, and be thou cast into the sea; and shall not doubt in his heart, but shall believe that those things which he saith shall come to pass; he shall have whatsoever he saith." – **Jesus, Mark 11:23**

*Date Set:*_____ *Date Accomplished/Received:*_____

I Will BELIEVE the Unbelievable and RECEIVE the Impossible...
MY POWER IS IN MY SAYING AND BELIEVING!

_____

_____

_____

_____

_____

_____

_____

_____

_____

_____

_____

_____

_____

_____

_____

_____

_____

_____

_____

_____

_____

_____

_____

_____

Date Set:_____ Date Accomplished/Received:_____

*"For verily I say unto you, That whosoever shall say unto this mountain, Be thou removed, and be thou cast into the sea; and shall not doubt in his heart, but shall believe that those things which he saith shall come to pass; he shall have whatsoever he saith." – **Jesus, Mark 11:23***

*Date Set:*_____ *Date Accomplished/Received:*_____

**I Will BELIEVE the Unbelievable and RECEIVE the Impossible...
MY POWER IS IN MY SAYING AND BELIEVING!**

_____

_____

_____

_____

_____

_____

_____

_____

_____

_____

_____

_____

_____

_____

_____

_____

_____

_____

_____

_____

_____

_____

*Date Set:*_____ *Date Accomplished/Received:*_____

*"For verily I say unto you, That whosoever shall say unto this mountain, Be thou removed, and be thou cast into the sea; and shall not doubt in his heart, but shall believe that those things which he saith shall come to pass; he shall have whatsoever he saith." – **Jesus, Mark 11:23**

Date Set:_____ Date Accomplished/Received:_____

**I Will BELIEVE the Unbelievable and RECEIVE the Impossible…
MY POWER IS IN MY SAYING AND BELIEVING!**

_____

_____

_____

_____

_____

_____

_____

_____

_____

_____

_____

_____

_____

_____

_____

_____

_____

_____

_____

_____

_____

_____

_____

*Date Set:*_____ *Date Accomplished/Received:*_____

*"For verily I say unto you, That whosoever shall say unto this mountain, Be thou removed, and be thou cast into the sea; and shall not doubt in his heart, but shall believe that those things which he saith shall come to pass; he shall have whatsoever he saith." – **Jesus, Mark 11:23**

_____
_____
_____
_____
_____
_____
_____
_____
_____
_____
_____
_____
_____
_____
_____
_____
_____
_____
_____
_____
_____
_____
_____
_____
_____

*Date Set:*_____ *Date Accomplished/Received:*_____

**I Will BELIEVE the Unbelievable and RECEIVE the Impossible…
MY POWER IS IN MY SAYING AND BELIEVING!**

_____
_____
_____
_____
_____
_____
_____
_____
_____
_____
_____
_____
_____
_____
_____
_____
_____
_____
_____
_____
_____
_____
_____

*Date Set:*_____ *Date Accomplished/Received:*_____

Give God thanks and praise EVERY day.

Even if it is a "sacrifice of praise" because things aren't going the way you want them to, do it as an act of faith. Remember that God is on your side. The Word is full of scriptures that give Him praise. Quote them. Remind yourself of His goodness and grace towards you. Remind yourself of what He has already done for you.

By giving God praise every day—making it part of your normal conversation—you are developing a habit of inspiring yourself by simply acknowledging the truth about God. The more you look at Him in the right way, the more hope will rise up in your heart and the more you will read His Word and have faith in it.

When true praise to God is a habit, your mindset will change and you will find yourself actually saying His Word with more than just a "wish" mentality. You'll start believing the "unbelievable" and that will cause you to receive the "impossible" things God promises throughout His Word. You can do this! Give God praise today—thank Him for what He *has* done, what He *is* doing, and for what you believe He *will* do in your life. That habit alone will keep you on the right road as you move between "the starting line" and "the finish line" of each and every dream, vision, or goal in life.

**I Will BELIEVE the Unbelievable and RECEIVE the Impossible…
MY POWER IS IN MY SAYING AND BELIEVING!**

_____

_____

_____

_____

_____

_____

_____

_____

_____

_____

_____

_____

_____

_____

_____

_____

_____

_____

_____

_____

_____

*Date Set:*_____ *Date Accomplished/Received:*_____

*"For verily I say unto you, That whosoever shall say unto this mountain, Be thou removed, and be thou cast into the sea; and shall not doubt in his heart, but shall believe that those things which he saith shall come to pass; he shall have whatsoever he saith." – **Jesus, Mark 11:23***

*Date Set:*_____ *Date Accomplished/Received:*_____

**I Will BELIEVE the Unbelievable and RECEIVE the Impossible…
MY POWER IS IN MY SAYING AND BELIEVING!**

_____
_____
_____
_____
_____
_____
_____
_____
_____
_____
_____
_____
_____
_____
_____
_____
_____
_____
_____
_____
_____
_____

*Date Set:*_____ *Date Accomplished/Received:*_____

*"For verily I say unto you, That whosoever shall say unto this mountain, Be thou removed, and be thou cast into the sea; and shall not doubt in his heart, but shall believe that those things which he saith shall come to pass; he shall have whatsoever he saith." – **Jesus, Mark 11:23***

Date Set:_____ Date Accomplished/Received:_____

**I Will BELIEVE the Unbelievable and RECEIVE the Impossible...
MY POWER IS IN MY SAYING AND BELIEVING!**

_____
_____
_____
_____
_____
_____
_____
_____
_____
_____
_____
_____
_____
_____
_____
_____
_____
_____
_____
_____
_____
_____
_____
_____
_____

*Date Set:*_____ *Date Accomplished/Received:*_____

*"For verily I say unto you, That whosoever shall say unto this mountain, Be thou removed, and be thou cast into the sea; and shall not doubt in his heart, but shall believe that those things which he saith shall come to pass; he shall have whatsoever he saith." – **Jesus, Mark 11:23***

_____
_____
_____
_____
_____
_____
_____
_____
_____
_____
_____
_____
_____
_____
_____
_____
_____
_____
_____
_____
_____
_____
_____
_____
_____

*Date Set:*_____ *Date Accomplished/Received:*_____

**I Will BELIEVE the Unbelievable and RECEIVE the Impossible…
MY POWER IS IN MY SAYING AND BELIEVING!**

_____

_____

_____

_____

_____

_____

_____

_____

_____

_____

_____

_____

_____

_____

_____

_____

_____

_____

_____

_____

_____

_____

_____

_____

_____

*Date Set:*_____ *Date Accomplished/Received:*_____

*"For verily I say unto you, That whosoever shall say unto this mountain, Be thou removed, and be thou cast into the sea; and shall not doubt in his heart, but shall believe that those things which he saith shall come to pass; he shall have whatsoever he saith." – **Jesus, Mark 11:23***

Date Set:_____ Date Accomplished/Received:_____

**I Will BELIEVE the Unbelievable and RECEIVE the Impossible…
MY POWER IS IN MY SAYING AND BELIEVING!**

_____
_____
_____
_____
_____
_____
_____
_____
_____
_____
_____
_____
_____
_____
_____
_____
_____
_____
_____
_____
_____

*Date Set:*_____ *Date Accomplished/Received:*_____

*"For verily I say unto you, That whosoever shall say unto this mountain, Be thou removed, and be thou cast into the sea; and shall not doubt in his heart, but shall believe that those things which he saith shall come to pass; he shall have whatsoever he saith." – **Jesus, Mark 11:23***

Date Set:_____ Date Accomplished/Received:_____

**I Will BELIEVE the Unbelievable and RECEIVE the Impossible…
MY POWER IS IN MY SAYING AND BELIEVING!**

_Date Set:_____ _Date Accomplished/Received:_____

You must have knowledge of what God is thinking about concerning you.

If you don't know, let me tell you now EXACTLY what God is thinking about when it comes to you: *"For I know the thoughts that I think toward you, saith the Lord, thoughts of peace, and not of evil, to give you an expected end"* (Jeremiah 29:11). If you aren't seeing the results you want, then you need to start quoting that scripture to yourself over and over again. I think one of the hardest things for a lot of Christians to do is to believe that God thinks good thoughts about them—maybe that's how you feel deep, down inside. If so, it's not your fault; it's the fault of wrong teaching.

For thousands of years, the Church has preached condemnation. The Church has told us that we couldn't change what we saw in our lives—we just had to take whatever came along. They taught us that everything good came from God and everything bad came from God, but that's just not true! Jesus came on the scene and told us the truth: There is a thief out there who comes to kill, steal, and destroy our lives, but that He came to give us LIFE so that we could have it in abundance (John 10:10).

God wants us to *know*, not just *believe*, that His thoughts about us are good. They are thoughts of peace. When you allow yourself to think that God is out to get you, then that is like saying He has evil thoughts towards you, and that is not true! There is no peace in that kind of thinking and God means for you to have peace (John 14:27). So, remind yourself regularly that God not only loves you, but He also has your BEST interests at heart. Be at peace knowing that He ONLY has thoughts of peace towards you!

**I Will BELIEVE the Unbelievable and RECEIVE the Impossible...
MY POWER IS IN MY SAYING AND BELIEVING!**

_____

_____

_____

_____

_____

_____

_____

_____

_____

_____

_____

_____

_____

_____

_____

_____

_____

_____

_____

_____

_____

*Date Set:*_____ *Date Accomplished/Received:*_____

*"For verily I say unto you, That whosoever shall say unto this mountain, Be thou removed, and be thou cast into the sea; and shall not doubt in his heart, but shall believe that those things which he saith shall come to pass; he shall have whatsoever he saith." – **Jesus, Mark 11:23***

Date Set:_____ Date Accomplished/Received:_____

**I Will BELIEVE the Unbelievable and RECEIVE the Impossible...
MY POWER IS IN MY SAYING AND BELIEVING!**

Date Set:_____ Date Accomplished/Received:_____

"For verily I say unto you, That whosoever shall say unto this mountain, Be thou removed, and be thou cast into the sea; and shall not doubt in his heart, but shall believe that those things which he saith shall come to pass; he shall have whatsoever he saith." – *Jesus, Mark 11:23*

_____

_____

_____

_____

_____

_____

_____

_____

_____

_____

_____

_____

_____

_____

_____

_____

_____

_____

_____

_____

_____

_____

_____

_____

_____

*Date Set:*_____ *Date Accomplished/Received:*_____

**I Will BELIEVE the Unbelievable and RECEIVE the Impossible…
MY POWER IS IN MY SAYING AND BELIEVING!**

_____
_____
_____
_____
_____
_____
_____
_____
_____
_____
_____
_____
_____
_____
_____
_____
_____
_____
_____
_____
_____
_____

*Date Set:*_____ *Date Accomplished/Received:*_____

*"For verily I say unto you, That whosoever shall say unto this mountain, Be thou removed, and be thou cast into the sea; and shall not doubt in his heart, but shall believe that those things which he saith shall come to pass; he shall have whatsoever he saith." – **Jesus, Mark 11:23***

_____

_____

_____

_____

_____

_____

_____

_____

_____

_____

_____

_____

_____

_____

_____

_____

_____

_____

_____

_____

_____

_____

_____

_____

_____

*Date Set:*_____ *Date Accomplished/Received:*_____

**I Will BELIEVE the Unbelievable and RECEIVE the Impossible...
MY POWER IS IN MY SAYING AND BELIEVING!**

_____
_____
_____
_____
_____
_____
_____
_____
_____
_____
_____
_____
_____
_____
_____
_____
_____
_____
_____
_____
_____
_____
_____
_____

Date Set:_____ Date Accomplished/Received:_____

*"For verily I say unto you, That whosoever shall say unto this mountain, Be thou removed, and be thou cast into the sea; and shall not doubt in his heart, but shall believe that those things which he saith shall come to pass; he shall have whatsoever he saith." – **Jesus, Mark 11:23***

*Date Set:*_____ *Date Accomplished/Received:*_____

**I Will BELIEVE the Unbelievable and RECEIVE the Impossible…
MY POWER IS IN MY SAYING AND BELIEVING!**

Date Set:_____ Date Accomplished/Received:_____

"For verily I say unto you, That whosoever shall say unto this mountain, Be thou removed, and be thou cast into the sea; and shall not doubt in his heart, but shall believe that those things which he saith shall come to pass; he shall have whatsoever he saith." – **Jesus, Mark 11:23**

_____

_____

_____

_____

_____

_____

_____

_____

_____

_____

_____

_____

_____

_____

_____

_____

_____

_____

_____

_____

_____

_____

_____

_____

*Date Set:*_____ *Date Accomplished/Received:*_____

**I Will BELIEVE the Unbelievable and RECEIVE the Impossible...
MY POWER IS IN MY SAYING AND BELIEVING!**

Date Set:_____ Date Accomplished/Received:_____

When God is your Helper, nothing is impossible for you!

Think about the reality of your salvation—that through the work of Jesus on the cross, God Almighty is living inside of *you*. You are born of His Spirit, so there is nothing too great for you to attempt or achieve. The truth is that whatever you think you "can't" achieve, you probably won't even attempt—but that is not the type of person God created you to be. This is why the Word instructs us to renew our mind to what God says. We do it to gain perspective. We do it to realize WHO we are in Christ…and to realize that with God, *nothing* is impossible.

You do your part and God will do His part. Remember Psalm 89:34: *"My covenant will I not break, nor alter the thing that is gone out of My lips."* I love that verse so much, I had it inscribed on my church building. Why? Because it shows me how much God thinks about His own Word. God *is* His Word. You can't separate Him from His Word (John 1:1)…and He will DO what He says He will do. Nothing is impossible with God. NOTHING!

**I Will BELIEVE the Unbelievable and RECEIVE the Impossible…
MY POWER IS IN MY SAYING AND BELIEVING!**

_Date Set:_____ _Date Accomplished/Received:_____

*"For verily I say unto you, That whosoever shall say unto this mountain, Be thou removed, and be thou cast into the sea; and shall not doubt in his heart, but shall believe that those things which he saith shall come to pass; he shall have whatsoever he saith." – **Jesus, Mark 11:23***

*Date Set:*_____ *Date Accomplished/Received:*_____

**I Will BELIEVE the Unbelievable and RECEIVE the Impossible…
MY POWER IS IN MY SAYING AND BELIEVING!**

_____

_____

_____

_____

_____

_____

_____

_____

_____

_____

_____

_____

_____

_____

_____

_____

_____

_____

_____

_____

_____

_____

_____

*Date Set:*_____ *Date Accomplished/Received:*_____

*"For verily I say unto you, That whosoever shall say unto this mountain, Be thou removed, and be thou cast into the sea; and shall not doubt in his heart, but shall believe that those things which he saith shall come to pass; he shall have whatsoever he saith." – **Jesus, Mark 11:23***

*Date Set:*_____ *Date Accomplished/Received:*_____

**I Will BELIEVE the Unbelievable and RECEIVE the Impossible…
MY POWER IS IN MY SAYING AND BELIEVING!**

_____

_____

_____

_____

_____

_____

_____

_____

_____

_____

_____

_____

_____

_____

_____

_____

_____

_____

_____

_____

_____

_____

_____

_____

*Date Set:*_____ *Date Accomplished/Received:*_____

"For verily I say unto you, That whosoever shall say unto this mountain, Be thou removed, and be thou cast into the sea; and shall not doubt in his heart, but shall believe that those things which he saith shall come to pass; he shall have whatsoever he saith." – **Jesus, Mark 11:23**

_____
_____
_____
_____
_____
_____
_____
_____
_____
_____
_____
_____
_____
_____
_____
_____
_____
_____
_____
_____
_____
_____
_____
_____
_____
_____

Date Set:_____ Date Accomplished/Received:_____

**I Will BELIEVE the Unbelievable and RECEIVE the Impossible...
MY POWER IS IN MY SAYING AND BELIEVING!**

_____

_____

_____

_____

_____

_____

_____

_____

_____

_____

_____

_____

_____

_____

_____

_____

_____

_____

_____

_____

_____

_____

_____

_____

_____

_____

*Date Set:*_____ *Date Accomplished/Received:*_____

"For verily I say unto you, That whosoever shall say unto this mountain, Be thou removed, and be thou cast into the sea; and shall not doubt in his heart, but shall believe that those things which he saith shall come to pass; he shall have whatsoever he saith." – **Jesus, Mark 11:23**

_____
_____
_____
_____
_____
_____
_____
_____
_____
_____
_____
_____
_____
_____
_____
_____
_____
_____
_____
_____
_____
_____
_____
_____
_____

*Date Set:*_____ *Date Accomplished/Received:*_____

**I Will BELIEVE the Unbelievable and RECEIVE the Impossible…
MY POWER IS IN MY SAYING AND BELIEVING!**

Date Set:_____ Date Accomplished/Received:_____

"For verily I say unto you, That whosoever shall say unto this mountain, Be thou removed, and be thou cast into the sea; and shall not doubt in his heart, but shall believe that those things which he saith shall come to pass; he shall have whatsoever he saith." – *Jesus, Mark 11:23*

_____
_____
_____
_____
_____
_____
_____
_____
_____
_____
_____
_____
_____
_____
_____
_____
_____
_____
_____
_____
_____
_____
_____

Date Set:_____ Date Accomplished/Received:_____

**I Will BELIEVE the Unbelievable and RECEIVE the Impossible…
MY POWER IS IN MY SAYING AND BELIEVING!**

_____
_____
_____
_____
_____
_____
_____
_____
_____
_____
_____
_____
_____
_____
_____
_____
_____
_____
_____
_____

*Date Set:*_____ *Date Accomplished/Received:*_____

True vision can never be destroyed.

Beware of sharing your vision—the dreams of your heart—with people of "lazy vision." Those are people who are always trying to make you see "reality" when, in fact, what they're really doing is trying to get you to be more like them: a hearer instead of a doer of God's Word.

Reality changes every moment. Life is in constant motion and so are we. The only thing that never changes is CHANGE. So, what's impossible today is a figment of your imagination. God can do anything you can believe Him for.

Keep your vision true. Keep saying to the mountain. Keep moving toward your goals. Don't let anybody tell you that you can't do it or won't make it. No! BE "God-inside minded." Think with the Word more than you think with your natural mind. Remember, empty people always seem to sound the loudest, and there is an echo coming out of their faithless hearts. But if you choose to throw off the religious mind and instead become God-inside minded, you're going to get to a place where you are not only *believing*, but also RECEIVING…and that's a place where all those "lazy vision" believers want to be but can't ever seem to go.

Don't let people who refuse to fight the good fight of faith fill you up with their words. Just smile. Focus on what you have to say and what you have to do. Keep filling your vessel full of the Word. Never ever forget that your power is in *your* saying and in *your* believing. Just like Jesus said, you *can* move mountains and have whatsoever *YOU* say.

**I Will BELIEVE the Unbelievable and RECEIVE the Impossible…
MY POWER IS IN MY SAYING AND BELIEVING!**

Date Set:_____ Date Accomplished/Received:_____

"For verily I say unto you, That whosoever shall say unto this mountain, Be thou removed, and be thou cast into the sea; and shall not doubt in his heart, but shall believe that those things which he saith shall come to pass; he shall have whatsoever he saith." – **Jesus, Mark 11:23**

_____
_____
_____
_____
_____
_____
_____
_____
_____
_____
_____
_____
_____
_____
_____
_____
_____
_____
_____
_____
_____
_____
_____
_____
_____

Date Set:_____ Date Accomplished/Received:_____

**I Will BELIEVE the Unbelievable and RECEIVE the Impossible...
MY POWER IS IN MY SAYING AND BELIEVING!**

Date Set:_____ Date Accomplished/Received:_____

"For verily I say unto you, That whosoever shall say unto this mountain, Be thou removed, and be thou cast into the sea; and shall not doubt in his heart, but shall believe that those things which he saith shall come to pass; he shall have whatsoever he saith." – **Jesus, Mark 11:23**

_____
_____
_____
_____
_____
_____
_____
_____
_____
_____
_____
_____
_____
_____
_____
_____
_____
_____
_____
_____
_____
_____
_____
_____
_____
_____
_____

Date Set:_____ Date Accomplished/Received:_____

**I Will BELIEVE the Unbelievable and RECEIVE the Impossible...
MY POWER IS IN MY SAYING AND BELIEVING!**

_____

_____

_____

_____

_____

_____

_____

_____

_____

_____

_____

_____

_____

_____

_____

_____

_____

_____

_____

_____

_____

_____

_____

_____

_____

*Date Set:*_____ *Date Accomplished/Received:*_____

"For verily I say unto you, That whosoever shall say unto this mountain, Be thou removed, and be thou cast into the sea; and shall not doubt in his heart, but shall believe that those things which he saith shall come to pass; he shall have whatsoever he saith." – **Jesus, Mark 11:23**

Date Set:_____ Date Accomplished/Received:_____

**I Will BELIEVE the Unbelievable and RECEIVE the Impossible...
MY POWER IS IN MY SAYING AND BELIEVING!**

_____
_____
_____
_____
_____
_____
_____
_____
_____
_____
_____
_____
_____
_____
_____
_____
_____
_____
_____
_____
_____
_____
_____
_____
_____

*Date Set:*_____ *Date Accomplished/Received:*_____

"For verily I say unto you, That whosoever shall say unto this mountain, Be thou removed, and be thou cast into the sea; and shall not doubt in his heart, but shall believe that those things which he saith shall come to pass; he shall have whatsoever he saith." – **Jesus, Mark 11:23**

_____

_____

_____

_____

_____

_____

_____

_____

_____

_____

_____

_____

_____

_____

_____

_____

_____

_____

_____

_____

_____

_____

_____

_____

_____

_____

Date Set:_____ Date Accomplished/Received:_____

**I Will BELIEVE the Unbelievable and RECEIVE the Impossible...
MY POWER IS IN MY SAYING AND BELIEVING!**

_Date Set:_____ _Date Accomplished/Received:_____

"For verily I say unto you, That whosoever shall say unto this mountain, Be thou removed, and be thou cast into the sea; and shall not doubt in his heart, but shall believe that those things which he saith shall come to pass; he shall have whatsoever he saith." – **Jesus, Mark 11:23**

_____
_____
_____
_____
_____
_____
_____
_____
_____
_____
_____
_____
_____
_____
_____
_____
_____
_____
_____
_____
_____
_____
_____
_____
_____
_____
_____

Date Set:_____ *Date Accomplished/Received:*_____

**I Will BELIEVE the Unbelievable and RECEIVE the Impossible…
MY POWER IS IN MY SAYING AND BELIEVING!**

_____
_____
_____
_____
_____
_____
_____
_____
_____
_____
_____
_____
_____
_____
_____
_____
_____
_____
_____
_____

*Date Set:*_____   *Date Accomplished/Received:*_____

Everything God asks you to believe is *un*believable. It's ALL impossible…that's why it's called faith. Just like nobody has the right or ability to steal your salvation, so you should never *give* other people the right or ability to steal the hopes, goals, and desires of your heart. God loves you. With Him, nothing is impossible for you to do. God is excited about your future. He knows exactly what you are capable of doing and becoming with Him…and He knows EVERY vision and dream of your heart. After all, how do you think those deep desires of your heart got there in the first place? God is a good God! He is the Author and Finisher of your faith and He *will* help you to accomplish and receive unbelievable and impossible things. Remember, dreams have NO expiration date. You can be sure that when those goals are complete—when those dreams or visions have come to pass—God will be right there with you, implanting new dreams and new visions into your heart for the future. There is NOTHING impossible for God, and that means there is nothing impossible for you. Keep your eyes on Him and remember: **Your power is in your saying and believing!**

"For verily I say unto you, That whosoever shall say unto his mountain, Be thou removed, and be thou cast into the sea; and shall not doubt in his heart, but shall believe that those things which he saith shall come to pass; he shall have whatsoever he saith."
  – Jesus, Mark 11:23

Other Books by Jesse Duplantis

Distortion: The Vanity of Genetically Altered Christianity

The Everyday Visionary

What in Hell Do You Want?

Wanting A God You Can Talk To

Breaking the Power of Natural Law

Jambalaya for the Soul

Heaven: Close Encounters of the God Kind
Also Available in Spanish & German

God Is Not Enough, He's Too Much!

The Ministry of Cheerfulness

Jesse's Mini-books

The Sovereignty of God

Running Toward Your Giant

Don't Be Affected by the World's Message

Keep Your Foot on the Devil's Neck

Leave It in the Hands of a Specialist

One More Night With the Frogs

The Battle of Life

Understanding Salvation
Also Available in Spanish

Available at www.jdm.org.